KARATE ON A CUSHION

A journey into Zen

Goran Powell

Foreword by Mike Eido Luetchford

KARATE ON A CUSHION
Copyright © 2020 Goran Powell
All rights reserved.
ISBN-13: 978-1981961955
ISBN-10: 198196195X

By the same author:

Non-fiction
Waking Dragons
Every Waking Moment

Fiction
A Sudden Dawn
Chojun
Matryoshka

*I beseech you, noble followers of Zen,
do not become so accustomed to images that
you are dismayed by the real dragon.*

Dogen, 1227

CONTENTS

Glossary of Terms

Foreword by Mike Eido Luetchford

1. Enter the Zendo
2. A New Sensei
3. Dogen Zenji
4. Fukanzazengi
5. Sitting Zazen
6. Balancing Body and Mind
7. A Philosophy of Action
8. The Buddha
9. Bodhidharma
10. Sudden Awakening
11. Ed and Laila
12. No Retreat
13. Anam Cara
14. Step Up, Stand Down
15. Genjo Koan
16. Beginner's Mind
17. Winter Camp
18. Zen and Karate
19. Kata by Numbers
20. Swindon Sesshin

21. Nature Preaches the Dharma
22. Empty Pages
23. No Mind
24. The Real Dragon
25. Karate on a Cushion

Appendix: Seki Shin Hen Pen – full poem and translation by Mike Eido Luetchford

Recommended Reading

Acknowledgements

GLOSSARY OF TERMS

Dan   Karate black belt levels

Dharma A word used in several ways, though all are related:
- Reality, universal truth, the world just as it is
- The Buddhist teachings or doctrine (on the universal truth)
- A thing – usually used in the plural: 'myriad dharmas' – all the things that go into making the universal whole

Eiheiji   Headquarters of the Soto Zen school, established by Dogen in 1244 and still in operation today

Koan   A Zen story, designed to help a student break out of delusion and see through to reality

Roshi   Honorific title, 'Master'

Sangha   Community, group of practitioners

Sensei   Teacher, instructor

Zazen   Seated Zen, meditation

Zendo   Meditation Hall, the place where zazen is practised

Zen   From the Chinese 'Chan' which comes from the Sanskrit 'Dyana', meaning 'breath'.

Zenji   Honorific title usually reserved for Dogen and meaning Zen Master

FOREWORD

More than forty years have passed since I first sat on a cushion, and I have continued sitting every day since that first experience. I had arrived in Japan in 1977 for a six-month work contract in Tokyo, and stumbled across this simple practice a few months after arriving. I was looking for something to fill my weekends with and noticed a small advertisement in a newspaper for a 'Zen seminar in English'. I knew nothing about Zen, and thought it would be interesting to find out.

I discovered that the way of Zen centred around a sitting practice called Zazen. The small Japanese man who was to become my teacher for the next four decades told me in his slow and primitive English that sitting in Zazen 'was action itself'. As a mountaineer and rock climber, I had already come to know the stillness that can be found sometimes at the very centre of committed action. I had occasionally entered a 'flow-like state' in which there was no 'me' climbing the 'rock': the rock and I were one. Experiencing that simple state had slowly become more important to me than getting to the top of the mountain, or climbing a new route. It had become a way of grounding myself in action that I had come to value and need.

Now, here in the middle of Tokyo, I found myself starting to practise and learn more about that simple state of balance and composure through the writings of a thirteenth century Japanese monk called Dogen. I am still practising and still learning.

In this excellent book, Goran tells us of his journey from karate to the meditation cushion, and how he has discovered what I had discovered – that the sitting practice called Zazen in Japanese is the essence of balanced action; the standard state of action. Later in the book, Goran describes the state of composure that he hoped to see in Ed and Laila during their 30 Man Kumite with phrases such as 'being in the zone' and 'no-mind', the state where our concentration is unbreakable and our conscious awareness is fully open. It is not related to winning or losing, but to being fully present, fully committed to the experience. It has been experience of this state that brought both me and Goran to the practice of sitting in zazen.

Realisation of this state has been carefully guarded and transmitted from teacher to student in an unbroken line of Buddhist teachers for more than 2000 years. Buddhism has acted as a vessel that has protected the teachings so that they are not diluted or distorted. Now we understand far more about our bodies and minds than the ancients did, and we have started to realise and experience ourselves, and how we act, more fully.

This realisation and experience of committed action does not belong only to Buddhism. It exists, and can be practiced, everywhere: in dance, in yoga, in sport, in music. Any committed sports practitioner will tell you that in the moment of action, winning or losing is not a factor and thinking is counter-productive. And in Zazen, we have been given a way to practise this state of committed action.

In the words of Dogen, *'If you practice the state like this for a long time, you will surely become the state like this itself. The treasure-house will open naturally, and you will be free to receive and to use its contents as you like.'*

Mike Eido Luetchford
January 2020

ENTER THE ZENDO

Some thirty years after first putting on a karate gi and learning to say 'Osu!' I was awarded my fifth dan black belt. It was an important moment for me, at once rewarding and more than a little daunting. Fifth dan is the first master grade. Did I feel like a master? In one sense, yes. I felt I understood karate through and through. I could talk about it for hours, going into great detail about any little thing, and I often did. I could teach black belts and junior instructors, and coach fighters through some gruelling tests. And yes, at fifty, I could still hold my own in hard sparring. But the word 'master' implies you've mastered a subject, and in no way did I feel I'd mastered karate. At best I had a deep understanding. I'd mastered the ability to perform at an advanced level. But to grasp the whole of karate felt way beyond my grasp.

This didn't bother me as much as you might think it should, because the ungraspable nature of karate is well known. The founder of my style, Chojun Miyagi, wrote how he felt he was walking blind on a path at night, trying to grasp the deeper meaning of his art. Today's renowned master Morio Higaonna likens his study of karate to attempting to grasp a cloud. My chief instructors, who are considerably further along the path than I am, are still seeking and developing. I share many moments with Sensei Gavin and his enthusiasm for learning is infectious. I meet with Sensei Dan several times a year and always pick up something new that leaves me inspired.

Soon after awarding me my master grade, Sensei Gavin began to introduce me to some of the things he'd been studying for some time. These included the more esoteric side of karate and its forerunner, Okinawan Te, namely the study of chi and vital points that can be used to injure or heal the body. And as part of this process, he recommended I should meditate regularly.

I'd already done some meditation in karate. Most styles incorporate five minutes here and there, often before or after a class. This usually involves kneeling with the eyes closed and focusing on deep breathing and keeping the mind clear. I was as familiar with this as the next man, but I was keen to delve more deeply into the link between Zen and the martial arts.

I'd been interested in Zen even before I knew what it was. Way back in the Seventies I would sit with my mum and watch Kung Fu on TV. Kwai Chang Caine, walking the earth in search of his long-lost brother, and kicking ass along the way. Almost more than the fight scenes (which in hindsight, were pretty lame) I loved the flashbacks to Grasshopper's lessons with old Master Po. It wasn't until years later that I realised the temple was Shaolin, the birthplace of Zen and martial arts.

I felt excited, as you do every time your sensei sets you a new challenge. I'd been given the green light to explore meditation in more depth. In truth, I don't think Gavin intended for me to visit a Zen group or study under a new teacher. He'd simply told me to add meditation to my own training. But I felt this was the moment I'd been waiting for – a chance to do something that had always been at the back of my mind. I'd read all about Zen and even written a novel about its first patriarch, Bodhidharma. I'd studied texts, sutras, translations, and koans. But I was like a swimmer who'd never been in the water. How much longer was I going to scout around the shoreline and dip my toes in the shallows? It was time to find a lake with a long pier and jump right in.

Earlier that year, I'd read a book called 'Eat, Sleep, Sit'. It was the autobiography of a Japanese salaryman who'd left the rat-race and joined Japan's most rigorous Zen monastery, Eiheiji. He'd spent a year doing little more than the title suggests: eating, sleeping, sitting, and staring at a wall. Something about the austerity of this appealed to me. It felt quite martial. I didn't think much of the beatings he took at the start – dished out by the trainer-monks to test his resolve. They sounded petty and cruel. But after 30 years of full-contact karate, I was confident I could handle the punishment, if it came to that.

So I began to look for a Zen group in London from the same lineage, and I found one called Dogen Sangha, named after master Dogen, the founder of Eiheiji.

On the website there were photos of people having tea and chatting in a small courtyard. They weren't dressed in formal robes and they looked like a friendly bunch. They certainly didn't look like they'd be dishing out a beating.

The teacher was a chap called Mike Luetchford, who'd studied for over twenty years in Japan with a master named Gudo Nishijima Roshi. Mike's credentials seemed impressive. I knew from experience in the martial arts that credentials aren't everything – and some aren't worth the paper they're printed on – but I had a good feeling about this group. The thing I liked most was that they concentrated on meditation rather than other practices like chanting or sewing or, heaven forbid, doing good deeds. I didn't have time for any of that. Meditation was what I wanted, and the Dogen Sangha seemed the place to start.

Only one thing really troubled me. I'd read that they sat for an hour at a time, with just one short walking-break halfway through. This seemed like an awfully long time.

I tried to meditate at home to prepare, starting with five minutes. It wasn't easy. On the day before my first visit, I decided to push it to fifteen minutes, but after what seemed like an eternity I grew fidgety and looked up at the clock. Six minutes had gone by. I got up, annoyed, and unable to face any more time alone with myself. I needed the discipline of a group to set me straight.

So it was with some trepidation that I packed loose tracksuit trousers instead of my usual karate gi the next day. Whether by chance or the mysterious workings of the Tao, I happened to be based in Tavistock Square, just minutes from where the group met on Wednesday nights. Strictly speaking, it was a karate night and I felt guilty for missing class. But I was determined to do this, and besides, this was part of my training.

By the time work finished, it was dark outside. Walking along Tavistock Street, past the 24-hour convenience stores and brightly lit kebab shops, I realised to my surprise

I was far more nervous about sitting on a cushion than I was about karate. What was I so worried about, I wondered? I guess I was afraid I'd fidget, or have my legs cramp up so badly that I'd be forced to give up and leave the room, annoying the others and causing a kerfuffle.

The group met in a multi-denominational church. I arrived at a church beside a modern glass-fronted building and rang the bell. An attendant arrived and when I asked about Zen meditation he directed me to the Buddhist Centre around the corner. Here I rang the bell and got no answer. I returned to the church that was, I felt sure, where the meditation took place. On further discussion, I was told the church I was looking for was the modern glass-fronted building next door. I suspected there was a lesson in there somewhere, but I didn't have time to figure it out.

Inside, I introduced myself to Tom, who'd arranged to meet me early and show me the ropes. Tom seemed friendly and welcoming, soft-spoken and unlikely to start dishing out a beating or making me wait outside for hours in the rain. He took me through to the meditation hall which was modern, with sleek black tiles and big panel windows showing through onto the patio courtyard. Only the smaller windows had little stained-glass scenes from the bible to remind us we were in a church. Beneath the window was a small statue of the Buddha in the lotus posture and a single candle. Around the edge of the room, black mats had been laid out, each with a cushion on top.

I'll share Tom's instructions with you now, just in case you ever find yourself in a similar situation, but keep in mind not all groups are the same and there will be differences. Anyway, here are the basics, so you don't embarrass yourself: first, leave your shoes outside. Keep your socks on if you like, but as a martial artist, it will feel strange and a bit wrong. Bowing is slightly different to entering a dojo. Rather than bowing in the doorway, step a little way into the room and imagine a circular path around it. This is roughly the path you will follow to get to your cushion. Standing on the edge of this imaginary path, press your palms together and bow in the direction of the Buddha statue. If this bothers you, don't think of it as worship but as a mark of respect, just like the martial arts.

Then take a definite step inside, turn to your left and walk, hand over fist, in a clockwise direction until you see a cushion that takes your fancy. If it looked like someone has prepared one specially (signified by the cushion being at the edge of the mat) avoid it and choose one in the middle. I sat on a cushion and tried to get both knees down firmly without success. After some experimentation, Tom suggested kneeling with a cushion beneath for support. A firm base is very important. I accepted this and asked about fidgeting. Tom said I should try and avoid it, but also not concern myself too deeply. We were just people sitting, he explained, so nothing to worry about. Nevertheless, I was determined to put in a good performance.

Taking my seat I shuffled about until I heard the bell ring three times to signal the beginning of the first bout. There was nothing for it, I was in and there was no going back. My mind was swimming with thoughts. Worse still, the blank wall that I was supposed to be staring at wasn't blank at all. There was a small black mark two inches to the left of centre. My eyes were so drawn to this spot that in the end I had to close them to stop looking at it.

Have you ever been in a train carriage when a party of school children gets on? That carriage was my mind! Class 3B was on its way to the Science Museum with a student teacher who's lost control and the chatter went something like this:

Hey, look at him, at the Zen dojo.
Doing his Zen.
I can't believe he's doing it.
Well I am, so give it a rest will you?
Ooh, hark at him!
No need to be rude.
What's gotten into him?
I'm trying to concentrate, that's what.
On what?
Nothing.
You're not supposed to concentrate.
I know!
You're supposed to just sit there and let mind and body fall away.
Yes, well how the hell am I supposed to do that with you lot jabbering on?
Okay, sorry.
But hang on a sec, what's that on the wall?
It's some sort of a black dot.

No, it's more like a kind of grubby little black mark.
Yes, I noticed that already. I'm trying to ignore it.
It's hard to ignore. Especially now that it's been pointed out.
Pity it's off-centre, or you could look at it.
Well it's not, so I can't.
That's a bit annoying, isn't it?
Not as annoying as some other things I could mention.
Hey, did you just close your eyes?
You're not supposed to close your eyes.
I'm telling the teacher.
The teacher can't see. No one can see me. I'm facing the wall. And this blasted black dot.
Mark.
Dot.
Mark.
Dot.
How many minutes do you think we've done?
About one.

Things went on and on like this until Tom mercifully sounded the bell. Despite the annoyance of the chatter, I felt a huge sense of achievement. I'd sat for twenty-five minutes without fidgeting and it was a new personal best by some considerable way.
We stood for five minutes of 'Kinhin' (slow walking) and I was expecting to be able to relax and stretch my legs. This hope was short-lived. The others were moving in super-slow motion using tiny steps and only going forward by

about half a foot's length each time. Their gazes were focused ahead and it seemed that even in walking they were in a state of meditation. I did my best to imitate them. After five minutes we'd only gone about five yards. Then Tom bowed and returned to his cushion to ring the bell. We returned to our seats at a more normal pace, still following the circular path.

I only had a few moments to prepare for the next sitting. This time I was determined to sit cross-legged in the hope that I would eventually become more flexible. I managed to get my left knee down solidly and propped a cushion under my right knee to support it. The bell sounded moments later and I was back in the hot seat. Class 3B re-entered in the carriage, but the initial excitement had worn off a bit. Still they kept up a steady chatter, talking the same old nonsense as before, until around twenty minutes had gone by. Then a new voice chimed in:

Hey, what's up with your foot?
It's just a bit hot.
Has it gone to sleep?
No, I can wiggle my toes.
It feels very hot. Try another wiggle.
It's fine, really.
Try it again.
Damn, now it's asleep.
That can be dangerous.
Really?
Yes! Remember that time you knelt on the wooden floor

for too long?
Yes.
And both your legs went to sleep?
Yes.
And when you tried to stand you nearly fell over?
Your point?
You could have broken your ankles.
Yes, but I didn't did I?
No but it could be dangerous.
Very dangerous.
And embarrassing.
So embarrassing.
You're right. I'm going to have to move.
Oh no, you can't move!
You promised you wouldn't.
Yes but this is serious.
I'm telling the teacher.
Tom is the teacher and he said it was OK.
Wimp.
Coward.
Loser.

I moved.

It was just a little fidget, to ease the pressure on my foot and get the circulation back and I don't think I disturbed the others too badly.
When we stood, I wiggled my toes and managed to leave the room upright with dignity intact.

Next, we sat at a table with tea and biscuits. I chose green tea because it seemed appropriate for Zen, then ruined it with a chocolate digestive.

I introduced myself to the group and tried hard to remember everyone's name. It's something I'm really bad at because, as my lovely wife keeps telling me, I'm not really interested in people. But today, I was – really interested! Because out of the eight million or so people in London, I'd found six who, like me, were interested in Zen, and I'd never met anyone like that before.

Next, we took turns reading paragraphs from a passage of Dogen's writings and Tom guided some discussion afterwards. The text was beautiful, poetic and puzzling. Members of the group were welcome to put forward their own views and interpretations. There was certainly no hard and fast doctrine that had to be learnt and maintained. I'd worried that I might be way out of my depth, so I was relieved to find most of the group were here to learn, just like me.

Leaving the church, I felt like I was walking on air. Was it just excitement and relief that I'd survived my first visit unscathed? An hour of sitting was possible without too much discomfort. The people were friendly and genuine. And no beatings! I was eager to get back in the saddle next week, when hopefully the novelty would begin to wear off and I could go deeper into my meditation.

The next day at work, I was still buzzing about my Zen experience and related it all rather breathlessly to my friend Adrian. He looked puzzled and asked how much I'd paid for the session.

'Five pounds,' I told him.

'You paid a fiver to stare at a wall?' he sniggered. 'You can come and do that at my place, if you like.'

A NEW SENSEI

The next week I was looking forward to meeting the teacher, Mike, who attended once a fortnight. In martial arts, finding the right sensei is so crucial that it's probably the single most important decision you will ever make. It's far more important than finding the right style. In our club, when students move to a new city, we advise them to find the best teacher and the most dynamic club, regardless of style. Forget about Goju Ryu karate and simply throw yourself into the training. This way you'll learn the heart of good martial arts – which is all the same – rather than sticking to a fixed ideology.

So when I returned to the Zen church, I was disappointed to learn that Mike sent his apologies but he'd missed a train and wouldn't be attending. Tom was showing another newbie the ropes, so I wasn't the newest any more.

Sitting this time, I didn't manage to get the cushions right before the bell and I was forced to remain in an uncomfortable position. This played on my mind and towards the end my foot went to sleep. I toughed it out and refocused my gaze on the wall, ignoring the discomfort as I'd trained to do in karate. However it wasn't a good sit.

After a slow walk around the hall, I grabbed an extra cushion on the way past and raised my seat, placing a third cushion beneath my knee to give me more support. Immediately I felt better, upright, rooted, poised and relaxed. Unsurprisingly, my mind managed to reach a much quieter and stiller place and my swings of thoughts weren't as extreme as before.

Afterwards, over tea and biscuits, we read a short passage by a senior monk in Japan about pain. The gist was that the mind can affect how badly you feel pain. Worrying about it makes it worse while accepting it makes it easier. I was pleased to see there were no fantastical claims about eliminating it with the power of the mind, just a well-reasoned argument about your approach to pain.

Someone in the group said I must know about pain from my karate. I was happy to share my thoughts on the subject, which were largely in line with the paper. If you keep thinking about your pain, you feel it more acutely than if you simply experience it and move on. What I didn't say (because it seemed a bit too aggressive for these nice people) was that if you focus on inflicting pain on your attacker, you hardly notice your own pain at all.

I did admit that in karate, we're trained to ignore pain and carry on. One lady pointed out, quite rightly, that pain is important to notify us of injuries, so we should take notice. This is valid, but only up to a point. If it's safe to do so, we can stop and attend to an injury. But if, for example, we're fighting for our lives, we need to ignore pain and fight on until the threat is over. The truth of the matter is we need to be flexible in our thinking, and able to react in different ways to the same stimulus. I think I demonstrated this rather well in my choice of a Garibaldi biscuit rather than the usual chocolate digestive.

Next week, Mike appeared – a tall, slender man of around 70, with short grey hair and a certain rigour in his bearing that I liked. I looked forward to hearing him speak after the sitting.

There were even more new people this time and the hall was almost full. I got three cushions set up just the way I liked and was sitting comfortably when I notice the chap next to me searching for a second cushion. The Buddha was testing me. Should I give up my third cushion and sit less comfortably? Or should I keep it and push for nirvana? In an act of infinite compassion, I handed over the cushion and shifted around until I was almost comfortable.

Both sessions before and after the slow-walking were marred by being uncomfortable and feet going to sleep. However it bothered me less than before. Towards the end, both feet went to sleep and I felt I was sitting in a warm wet puddle. A bit like a baby must feel in a full nappy. I tried to laugh it off and refocus on the wall. At least there was one good thing – no black dot this week.

After a shaky exit, we gathered in the canteen and Mike spoke about zazen – which translates as 'seated Zen' or simply 'meditation'. He had a simple way of talking that I liked. He offered no great revelations and promised no wonderful rewards. The benefits of sitting on a cushion and staring at a wall were simply that we got to sit on a cushion and stare at the wall. In the frantic pace of modern life, we're bombarded by thoughts from morning till night. And when we go to sleep, there's no rest, because our thoughts turn into dreams. But here's an hour to spend doing something very simple and fundamental.

Mike's approach was straightforward and his speech vivid. He seemed able to take enigmatic passages of Zen prose and make them clear and understandable. Most of all, I liked his pragmatic attitude. I hadn't come here expecting miracles, just some guidance to begin my practice and deepen my understanding, and I felt Mike might be just the man for this.

He seemed to find questions about enlightenment faintly ridiculous and refused to be drawn into discussions. Mindfulness was all the rage and people were being promised enlightenment experiences in an afternoon. The similarities with martial arts were all too clear. Rather than achieving some sort of 'other state' outside our own experience, Mike seemed more interested in achieving balance in the here and now. Not a sort of neutral middle ground but rather a suppleness of body and mind that was free to go where it wanted.

Over the next few months I got to learn a bit more about Mike and his background. He'd gone to Japan in 1977 and shortly after arriving, had attended a lecture by a Japanese monk, Gudo Nishijima, who was interested in teaching Zen to Westerners. At the time the Beatles were experimenting with transcendental meditation and Zen sounded pretty cool. Mike tried zazen and felt something

profound from sitting, something akin to the feelings he got from one of his existing passions, mountain climbing.
One of our group asked whether Mike had shopped around and investigated other schools of Buddhism. Mike said he hadn't. He'd been satisfied with the teaching he'd got, especially since Nishijima Roshi taught in English, which was rare. At first the teachings had been hard to grasp but over the years, they'd sunk in.
I liked this answer. In martial arts there's far too much shopping around. With transport and technology as they are, we can train with the most famous masters in the world. It's very tempting to build up a who's-who résumé of big names that you've trained under. But real progress comes from knuckling down with one teacher in one discipline for a concerted time. Find a sensei you trust and, like it or not, do as they say. Our biggest leaps come from doing the things we like least of all. I speak from experience.
I soon came to like and admire Mike and consider him a sensei who could teach me a great deal. The thing I liked most was that he promised so very little. In fact, nothing at all. He never held out any incentive of any kind. No enlightenment or nirvana or anything particularly special. Just a flavour of something that, he said, 'speaks to him'. And because he kept things really simple, and true, and seemed to return to the same key messages over and over – something I know to be important from the martial arts.
Mike said many Westerners have a rose-tinted view of Zen. They see a mystical experience set in beautiful

temples on mist covered mountains – which is all very nice but nothing to do with reality. I was a bit disappointed to hear this because I love temples on mist-covered mountains. I'd secretly hoped for just a little bit of this – a tiny touch of Zen mystery and magic. But Mike wasn't peddling any of that, and in my heart, I knew he was right. Zen is about reality, here and now, not some imaginary 'other life' or 'better place' that we can access through meditation. So I waved goodbye to cherry blossoms blowing like snowflakes in temple courtyards in favour of getting a better handle on reality.

Mike didn't stop there. He went on to say the whole idea of Zen being a spiritual practice was a red herring, and 'spirituality' was a word best avoided. I was taken aback by this because surely Zen – like karate – is all about spirit? Apparently not. Sitting in zazen is about mind and body, which are one, inseparable. And both real. Spirit can be taken to mean something mystical which may or may not exist and leads us away from reality. Again, I got it.

Mike also seemed to find the whole Zen austerity thing faintly ridiculous. Sitting in zazen is challenging enough, especially for long periods, as I was discovering. He wasn't averse to making sustained effort and pushing through discomfort. But he found the idea of sitting all night or striking each other with sticks quite laughable. The effort required to stay alert and maintain a good posture is an exercise in itself. The motivation is best coming from you, naturally, rather than from the threat of a big stick.

Again, I felt Mike was right. In good karate there is hard

training, however it only feels like austerity for a while. That's because most of us are used to a rather soft way of living. The idea of doing knuckle push-ups and striking one another seems harsh. But over time it becomes the norm and our boundaries get reset. The real truth is that modern living is so comfortable that a little austerity does us the world of good. Compared to our ancestors, who walked for miles, toiled in fields and carried heavy loads, we barely use our bodies. Our muscles waste and our hearts and lungs grow weak through lack of effort. What we think of as hardship is only using our bodies as they were meant to be used. By the time we reach middle age, we should consider it a privilege (not a chore) to be able to run, jump, kick and squat without doing ourselves a mischief.

One evening Mike showed us a lineage chart for our group. In martial arts and in Zen, the idea of lineage – a plotted history of teachers stretching back to the founder – is considered important. Personally, I'm only mildly interested in these charts because irrespective of what it says on paper, it's the present-day teaching that really matters. Nevertheless, I was delighted to see that our group's lineage stretched all the way back to Bodhidharma, and from there it was just a short hop, via 27 Indian patriarchs, to the Buddha.

In case you don't know it, Bodhidharma, as well as being considered the first patriarch of Zen in China, is also credited with establishing martial arts at the Shaolin Temple. These days, modern martial arts historians have largely disproved this as literary licence. Some even question his existence. But this didn't matter to me. For some time I'd been content to view Bodhidharma's story not as fact but rather as allegory, a sort of moral guidance. Something to inspire our behaviour today.

Much of Zen's history seems allegorical. The original Buddha was a prince who gave up a kingdom to discover the truth and seek an end to suffering. Bodhidharma was from a noble family and gave up everything to follow the way. He sat in meditation for so long that his legs fell off. He cut off his own eyelids to prevent himself from falling asleep. His disciple stood all night in the snow to show his sincerity but Bodhidharma was unimpressed. Only after the man cut off his own arm did Bodhidharma take notice. We're not meant to take all this literally. We're meant to realise that we don't get anything worth having without sacrifice. Or by continuing to do what we already do. To change ourselves, we must give up part of who we are. This begins by changing our behaviour in some significant way, right now. Easy to say. Hard to do.

Seeing Bodhidharma's name in the lineage chart brought into focus something I'd been searching for – a vague idea at the back of my mind. Now I could trace two different paths back to Bodhidharma, one through my martial arts and the other through Zen. The martial arts lineage was much less defined. From my own teachers to Chojun Miyagi, the founder of our style, was easy enough to follow. Miyagi's teacher Kanryo Higaonna trained in southern Chinese martial arts, and pretty much all of these claim a lineage back to Shaolin. These claims are, for the most part, impossible to verify. But that's not the point. The reason for the claims tells us something important. These fighting arts aspire to originate in a monastery rather than a sports arena, or a battlefield.

Two different routes came from Bodhidharma to where I was today. One through kicking and punching, the other through sitting on a cushion and staring at a wall. Two roads leading from the same place. What were the differences? What were the connections? And did the two ever join and become a dual carriageway? I realised I had some fascinating exploring to do.

DOGEN ZENJI

Almost everything we studied in the Dogen Sangha was written by Master Dogen, the 13th century monk who founded Soto Zen, one of the largest schools in Japan.

Born in 1200AD, Eihei Dogen was a child prodigy who began studying Buddhism at a young age. His father died when he was two and his mother when he was seven. Dogen joined a monastery at twelve. His talent for language meant he'd read the Chinese classics and studied with the greatest masters of his time. However one question bothered him and he couldn't find an answer to it. The study of Buddhism is usually associated with an awakening to reality called enlightenment. But it's also said that we're already perfect as we are, so there's no need to awaken to anything. Dogen's question, quite understandably, was this: if we are perfect as we are, why do we need to practice? Dogen put this question to the senior monks at the temple and didn't feel he got a satisfactory response. He visited other temples and masters and still got no answer that he could accept. Finally he heard a saying from Eisai, the master who founded the Rinzai school of Zen, who said he didn't know about enlightenment but he did know white cats and donkeys.

This is a typical Zen story – the sort of thing you need to get used to if you're going to get the hang of how Zen is communicated. What Eisai basically said was be couldn't answer intellectual problems that young monks were agonising over but he did know what was right in front of him – reality. We can imagine a white cat and a donkey outside the window and Eisai pointing at them. Direct pointing at reality. Dogen liked this answer better than any other and stayed on to study at Eisai's temple.

This is a recurring theme in Zen koans. The master steers the student away from intellectual agonising to simply seeing reality as it is. The real world doesn't exist as a series of precariously assembled thoughts in our minds. It is real, right in front of us. We can see it, plain as day, just by looking at it. However as soon as we start 'thinking' about what we're seeing, we are no longer looking in real time but rather we have taken a series of snapshots that we are now analysing (often to death) in our own minds.

This is a theme we'll come back to again and again because it really is at the heart of Zen. And karate. In the Zen stories (koans) the student approaches the master with a question and seeks an answer that is intellectually satisfying. The master slaps the student in the face, sometimes literally, or at least verbally. The first and most obvious message is: stop bothering me with your annoying intellectual agonisings. The second, more important message is this: you already know the answer, it's right in front of you. Reality is unfolding before you, and me, and all of us, at every moment. You've been alive all this time. You've had all these experiences. Do you really need me to tell you what to do? Or how to think? How much longer are you going to keep coming to me with questions instead of just getting on with it?

There's a moment of silence, then questions begin again. Getting on with... what? The master can barely resist another slap.

Eisai died a year later and his temple was taken over by a senior monk, Myozen. Dogen studied with Myozen but he still didn't feel he'd penetrated his subject to the core. Apparently Myozen didn't either, and the two of them travelled together to China to get to the heart of the matter.

Dogen was disappointed in the temples in China and spent several years in search of a true master. On the verge of giving up and returning to Japan, he heard of a great master named Tendo Nyojo and went to study with him. Here his doubts were quickly cleared and finally, the great question was answered for him.

When pressed on what he'd learnt in China, Dogen's answer was simply that he'd returned with 'a flexible mind'. This implies that rather than neat answers to all his questions, he'd learnt to view things differently and was no longer hung up on them. Nevertheless his original question remained a recurring theme in his writing which he addressed in some of his most famous pieces, as we'll see later.

On his return to Japan, Dogen joined a temple in the capital Kyoto, but soon found that he wanted to do things his own way. He moved outside the capital and began to give lectures to a small group of monks. His return to the fundamentals – meditation – and the simple truth at the heart of his message, made him popular. This in turn made him unpopular with rival Buddhist sects who vied for prominence in the capital. For the sake of peace, and his personal safety, he moved to a remote mountain on the north coast by the Sea of Japan, and founded the temple named after him: Eihei-ji. The temple still stands today and remains the headquarters of Soto Zen. Young monks still eat, sleep and sit, while tourists are welcome to explore the beautiful buildings and gardens.

Dogen's style of Zen had a back-to-basics approach that went against the grain at the time. He asserted that the Buddha awakened to reality by meditating and that Bodhidharma sat for nine years at Shaolin. Other practices such as studying the scriptures and solving koan puzzles were useful, but meditation was essential, and he felt it had been relegated too far in other schools.

Ironically, considering his emphasis on meditation rather than scripture, Dogen was a prolific writer. In his lifetime he penned 95 chapters in a collection called Shobogenzo –

'The Treasury of the True Dharma Eye' – covering every conceivable aspect of Buddhist life from meditation and doctrine to history, observations, commentaries on ancient texts, and long lists of rules and regulations for the monastery. In this vast collection there are passages that soar with beautiful imagery and deliver piercing insights one after another. There are passages filled with fastidious rules and regulations regarding a monk's conduct, instructions to the Tenzo (cook) on how to prepare food, and to diners on how to clean their bowls after eating. There are even detailed instructions on how to wipe (both 'front' and 'back') after going to the toilet.

If 95 chapters wasn't enough, Dogen wrote other pieces that are often incorporated into the Shobogenzo, most notably his instructions on how to sit in meditation titled Fukanzazengi, and a medieval Q&A called Bendowa, in which he poses a set of frequently-asked-questions and answers them, explaining and justifying his methods as the authentic way passed down by the ancestors. And while he didn't believe koan practice was essential for enlightenment, he collected them with a passion and compiled a book of 301 koans called Shinji Shobogenzo.

His writing reveals the full extent of the man. Dogen can be scathing, nit-picking, pedantic and monumentally arrogant. He's not above relating stories of great masters and then suggesting how they could have done things better. He can take a subject and analyse it to death, present it every which way, and contort logic and words until your head hurts. His writing can be so dense as to be practically unintelligible, so filled with contradictions that you simply throw the book down in frustration. And then... he can capture something so profound with such beauty, brevity and clarity that the effect, at least for me, is breath-taking. Even in translation, which always makes things a bit clunky, there's a poetry to his style and a use of imagery that transports you.

One of the words we hear most frequently in Dogen's writing is 'Dharma', which has quite a few meanings, the most important of which is 'reality' or the way the universe really is. Reality is ineffable – it cannot be fully described in words, nor conceived in the mind. After all, we exist within reality, as part of it, so we cannot wholly contain something that wholly contains us, except as a concept in our minds. It's like a fish, swimming in the ocean, thinking about the ocean. The ocean in the fish's mind isn't the real ocean.

Having said that, Dogen does as good a job of expressing the inexpressible as you're ever likely to get. And for this reason, as well as many other, he's still widely regarded as the first and finest source on Zen. The title 'Zenji' simply means Zen Master. And he's also arguably Japan's greatest philosopher.

Dogen's writings lay dormant for hundreds of years, being almost as difficult for Japanese people to understand as for Westerners, until they gained new interest in the twentieth century.

Mike's teacher, Gudo Nishijima, first came across Dogen in a book on the spiritual history of Japan that was considered essential reading. Intrigued by what he learned about Dogen, he sought out The Shobogenzo to read the master's original work. Though young at the time, he considered himself an able scholar, so he was astonished to find he couldn't understand a single word of Dogen's so-called masterpiece. And yet... he felt the text spoke to him profoundly, and began to study with a Zen master named Kodo Sawaki. He was deeply impressed with Kodo Sawaki's teachings and settled down to study the Shobogenzo in great depth. Over many years he came to understand more and more until finally, he got it.

Nishijima felt Buddhism in Japan had stagnated and like several of his well-known contemporaries, he turned to a Western audience. The world was, he believed, based on Western systems of logic, philosophy and commerce, and Western views tend to be polarised. We either believe in science or religion. We are either materialistic or spiritual. It's all or nothing. Nishijima felt Dogen's brand of Buddhism offers a valuable 'Middle Way' between two extremes and fills an important gap.

Since he spoke good English, he decided the best way to get this message across would be to translate Dogen's masterpiece for a Western audience. He also began to lecture in English to a small group of Westerners, including Mike – who went on to study with him for over 20 years. Several other students have now gone on to be teachers in their own right, most notably Brad Warner, who writes some wonderfully accessible books about Zen and Dogen.

With the help of his English-speaking students, Nishijima began the monumental task of translating the Shobogenzo. Many years later, the task was complete, in four volumes, each the size of a normal paperback. There's no doubt Nishijima Roshi made an enormous contribution to Western understanding of Dogen. His book 'To Meet the Real Dragon' gives a personal account of his views after a lifetime of study and is also recommended reading.

FUKANZAZENGI

In any collections of Dogen's major works, there's one passage that's sure to appear. In fact, any book that says anything about Zen meditation is likely to quote from it. Called 'Fukanzazengi' – The Universal Guide to the Standard Method of Zazen – it's the original and pretty much impossible to improve upon.

Although it was not written as part of the Shobogenzo, it is often included as an appendix and it feels very much at home with Dogen's other writings. So for everything you need to know about zazen, and more, here's what the great man has to say:

The truth is all around us. Why do we need to practice sitting to awaken to it? The way to enlightenment comes naturally. Why make special effort to attain it? We are perfect as we are. Why attempt to polish ourselves until we shine?

All this may be so. But if there is the slightest gap, then this gap is as big as the divide between heaven and earth.

Even if you're already enlightened, with deep insight, able to see the truth at a glance with a clear mind, you're only half way there – still playing in the gateway instead of walking the path.

The Buddha was wise from birth but even so, he sat for six years and the effects still resonate today. Bodhidharma had already received mind-to-mind transmission before he famously sat for nine years facing a wall. If the ancient sages did this, how can we dispense with wholehearted practice today?

So put aside intellectual pursuits like studying words and chasing meanings. Take a backward step and shine the light inwards. Body and mind will fall away and your original nature will manifest. If you want this to happen then get to work on it right now.

Find a quiet room to practice zazen. Eat and drink in moderation. Cast aside all involvements and suspend all affairs. Forget about good and bad, right and wrong. Give up all thinking, intellectual pondering and even consciousness itself. Stop measuring with thoughts, ideas, and views. Have no designs on becoming a buddha. How can sitting make you a buddha?

Spread out a thick mat and put a cushion on it. Sit either in the full-lotus or half-lotus position. In the full-lotus, first place your right foot on your left thigh, then your left foot on your right thigh. In the half-lotus, simply place your left foot on your right thigh. Tie your robes loosely and arrange them neatly. Then place your right hand on your left leg and your left hand on your right palm, thumb-tips lightly touching.

Straighten your body and sit upright, leaning neither left nor right, forward nor backward. Align your ears with your shoulders and your nose with your navel. Rest the tip of your tongue against the front of the roof of your mouth, with teeth together and lips shut. Keep your eyes open and breathe softly through your nose.

Once you are settled in your posture, take a breath and exhale fully. Rock your body right and left, and settle into the mountain-still state. Then think about not thinking. What kind of thinking is not-thinking? Non-thinking. This is the crux of zazen.

Sitting in zazen is not Zen concentration. It is simply the dharma gate to joyful ease. The practice-and-experience that brings to life the awakened state. The universe is realised without restriction. To grasp this is to be like a dragon returning to water, or a tiger in its mountain stronghold. Remember, the true Dharma is always naturally manifesting itself before us, and when you are sitting properly, darkness and distraction drop away.

When you rise from sitting, move slowly and quietly, calmly and deliberately. Do not rise suddenly or abruptly. If we look into the past, we see that those who transcended the mundane life and indeed the spiritual life all did so through zazen.

The triggering of awakening with a finger, a banner, a needle, or a mallet, and the bringing of realisation with a whisk, a fist, a staff, or a shout – these (koan stories) cannot be understood by discriminative thinking. Much less can they be known by achieving mystical powers. They represent a way of acting that comes before knowledge and views.

Intelligence, or lack of it, is not an issue. Make no distinction between dull and sharp-witted people. If you concentrate your effort single-mindedly, that in itself is wholeheartedly engaging the way. Practice-realisation is naturally undefiled. Going forward becomes an everyday affair.

All the patriarchs of India and China sat like the Buddha, and while each lineage has its own style, they are all united in their devotion to sitting in zazen. Although they say there are ten thousand distinctions and a thousand variations, they all wholeheartedly engage in the way through zazen.

Why look for anything else? Why leave the seat in your own home to wander in vain through the dusty realms of other lands? One false step and you stumble past what is directly in front of you.

You have been given human form, which is a great opportunity. Don't pass your days in vain. Perform the essential activity of the Buddha-way (zazen) rather than taking momentary delight in things that glitter and sparkle.

The body is like a dewdrop on a blade of grass. Life passes like a flash of lightning. Suddenly it is gone. In an instant it is lost.

I beseech you, noble followers of Zen, do not become so accustomed to images of a mythical dragon that you are dismayed when you encounter a real one.

Devote your energies to the way of direct pointing at the truth. Revere those who have gone beyond learning and are free from effort. Accord with the enlightenment of the buddhas and become a rightful successor to the patriarchs. Live in such a way, and you will be such a person. The treasure store will open naturally and you will be able to enjoy it freely.

SITTING ZAZEN

Considering Dogen's ultimate guide to zazen was written 800 years ago, the instructions are remarkably clear and true today. Notice how he begins by stating, and then answering, his own question – the one that troubled him for so long as a young monk:

The truth is all around us. Why do we need to practice sitting to awaken to it? The way to enlightenment comes naturally. Why make special effort to attain it? We are perfect as we are. Why attempt to polish ourselves until we shine?'

Dogen dangles the carrot in front of us before whisking it away. The truth is right in front of us, but we're so full of our own bullshit that we can't see it. To be fully awakened to reality is to see things as they really are, moment by moment, without the slightest mental filter. Without accepting or rejecting things according to our existing beliefs. To see the world with such clarity is difficult enough for a master, let alone a student.

No one, master or student, can see reality with perfect clarity all the time. Now and then, more often than not, there will be a slight disconnect – a 'gap' as Dogen calls it – between what we see and what we interpret. And as soon as this gap opens, it makes all the difference in the world.

This gap can and will open up at any time for all of us and there's nothing we can do to stop it. But we can get better at noticing it and closing it. We can learn to go for longer periods without it opening up. Through regular practice we get better at sealing up the gap for a few seconds, a few minutes, or a few hours at a time.

Serious martial artists will be familiar with this gap. One minute you're in the zone, in the middle of a kata, performing everything just right. The next, a stray thought pops into your head – a question, a worry, a doubt. Then you lose it. You falter. Or you're fighting in a tournament and doing perfectly well, until a stray thought enters your head and pops, like a bubble, leaving a gooey mess. Your opponent starts scoring. You start second guessing. You can't seem to catch up with what's going on. Any second now you're going to wake up on the floor with the referee slapping your face and asking if you know your own name – believe me, I've been there.

Dogen goes on to say that even if you're enlightened you still need to practice every day. The original masters, Buddha and Bodhidharma, sat for years and continued to sit, so who are we to think we needn't bother? If you want to experience what they experienced, then stop messing about (or shopping around) and get on with it.

... put aside intellectual pursuits like studying words and chasing meanings. Take a backward step and shine the light inwards. Body and mind will fall away and your original nature will manifest. If you want this to happen then get to work on it right now.

Body and mind 'falling away' is another of Dogen's best-known and most beautiful phrases, taken from his master in China, Tendo Nyojo.

As a martial artist, have you ever felt as if your body and mind fell away? Not literally, but as if you were so engaged in what you were doing that there was no separation between you and your opponent, or you and your kata? Not the slightest gap? I have, occasionally. These are the moments when we're in the zone, 'in the flow state', immersed in a kata or sparring without the slightest delay. This is something that I have been able to develop over the years, and I got better at it gradually, from simply cultivating this way of training and doing it more often, and longer each time.

As a young fighter I would fire a lot of punches and kicks in roughly the direction of my opponent in the hope that some would land. As I got better, I learnt to pick my shots and hit intended targets. But the real change came when I began to read my opponent. Reading means not just seeing openings as they occur but predicting them. This comes from recognizing movements that will lead to an opening a nanosecond later, and throwing strikes in advance.

Nowadays, this is how I manage to keep pace with younger, faster fighters. But to do so I need to connect with my opponent rather than set myself against him. I do this by forgetting about my own kicks and punches and instead watching his movements, not just now and then but the whole time. My punches and kicks have learnt to strike openings without being told. In this way I'm no longer conscious of my own body but rather, I'm inhabiting my opponent's movements.

It sounds a bit strange saying it like this, but it's nothing particularly special or unusual. It's also not fool-proof and doesn't always work. It's just what advanced fighters do. It's the concept behind styles like judo and aikido that purport to use an opponent's strength against him. But in truth, all fighting arts work this way at an advanced level. In boxing, it's counter-punching – waiting for the opponent to drop his guard and open up before attacking. But how can you use your opponent's strength against him if you're not prepared to forget yourself and pay attention to his actions?

If 'body and mind falling away' is being wholly engaged in the action, then thinking does nothing but get in the way. In my own experience, whenever I've entertained a thought that wasn't directly related to the action of the fight, I've suffered.

In my very first full-contact 'knockdown' match, I was doing well against a much more experienced opponent, until the moment I thought, 'I'm doing well against a much more experienced opponent.' At that moment I didn't see a shot that I should have noticed – and would have noticed if I'd remained wholly engaged in the fight – and got caught with a vicious liver shot that put me on the ground. Mentally stepping outside the action and into 'assessment' is a very common and very dangerous gap. There is a time for assessment, before or after, but not during a performance. I will go into more detail about staying in the game later. Dogen goes on to give us classic instructions on how to sit in zazen. In karate we normally meditate in the kneeling position, with the eyes closed, and we often count breaths. I believe the samurai preferred to meditate kneeling because it's easier to stand up and start cutting if a ninja should happen to burst through your wall and try to kill your master.

However in zazen we sit facing a wall with our backs to the world (which the samurai wouldn't like either). The eyes are half open and there's no instruction from Dogen to focus on breathing. In a chapter called Shikantaza, he talks again about zazen and emphasises that it is not a means to an end but quite simply all we need. Shikantaza means something like 'wholeheartedly just sitting'. There is no intention of sitting leading to anything special or attaining any particular new power or insight. Simply by sitting – without thinking, or trying 'not to think' – we put ourselves in a pre-conceptual state and experience reality just as it is, without adding our own mental constructs.

Whether we sit or kneel, count breaths or not, open or close the eyes, the exercise is the same – to stay present in the moment without adding an extra layer of thought to the experience. Anyone who has tried meditating even for a minute or two will know how difficult this can be. Thoughts bubble up constantly like the magic porridge pot that never stops producing thick, gloopy porridge.

What at first seems like the simplest of instructions – 'just sit' – becomes one of the most challenging things you can attempt. Because like the naughty schoolboy who's told to sit still outside the head-teacher's office, we just can't. Our minds need to fidget. I know mine does. Hell, yes! A rapier-like intellect like mine can't be constrained and wasted on something as simple as sitting. It has to think about things: temples on mist covered mountains, pondering the words of Dogen, karate strategy, tactics and techniques. And whole chapters of interesting stuff to write in my next book.

But Dogen is adamant: just sit. He gives us clear instruction on the physical aspect of sitting. Perhaps surprisingly for us Westerners, the lotus position is not meant to be a torment to endure but rather a posture that enables someone to sit firmly and comfortably for long periods. I guess it helps to be born in a culture where kneeling, squatting and sitting on the floor are more common, so the emphasis on full or half lotus is not insisted upon in most Western groups. Rather, the aim is to achieve a firm base created by a triangle that consists of your butt and your two knees, which should be firmly connected to the ground on a comfortable mat, and this triangular base can be achieved through sitting or kneeling. In the Dogen Sangha, those who can sit cross-legged are encouraged to do so because it opens the sacroiliac joint between the pelvis and the lower spine. If you can place one or both feet up on the other leg, that's great. However, if this isn't possible then kneeling is permitted. In this case, it's best to raise the weight off your ankles by popping a zafu (cushion) between your legs, or your feet will quickly go to sleep. Turning the cushion on its edge also helps, so your feet aren't splayed too wide. Some people bring a specially designed wooden bench that they sit on and tuck their legs beneath.

Sometimes I've managed the half-lotus but most times I sit in what is called the Burmese style which is basically cross-legged with both knees on the mat, or supported by a thin cushion. I've tried leaving the knee hanging in the hope that it will stretch down under its own weight. However over 25 minutes, it puts a strain on the hips and throws your whole posture out. It's better to pop a support under your knee and lower it as you get more supple.

In my own sitting I find it takes fifteen minutes to reach my most open and relaxed state. Another five minutes is usually fine but after that, one or both feet start going to sleep and things get a bit more difficult.

Once we're sitting, Dogen tells us to move around until we find our central balance. The feeling is as if the vertebrate of the spine are neatly stacked, one on top of the other, with the head resting naturally on top of the pile. Those familiar with the Sanchin posture of Goju Ryu (or similar) will recognise that essentially, the top half of the body is the same in Sanchin and zazen, and only the legs have changed. Both are a relaxed, balanced, rooted posture.

The sitting environment is deliberately neutral. Dogen recommends a room that's quiet, not too hot or too cold, a blank wall, and as few distractions as possible. The eyes remain open because closing them tends to stimulate the imagination and encourage daydreaming. Keeping the eyes open keeps us where we are, in the room, just sitting.

The eyes are half-open and cast slightly downwards to avoid straining. This half-open style keeps them moist and relaxed so we can hold this gaze for long periods. In short, Dogen is stacking all the odds in our favour. He is making it as comfortable as he can for us and giving us the least amount of distractions. Surely now we can 'just sit'? Well, we can try.

No matter where you sit, there will always be some distractions. Bells ringing. Traffic honking. People walking around outside. Flies buzzing. Other people in the room, clearing their throats or shuffling on their cushions. Don't let this bother you. The things going on around us are reality. We're not trying to escape from it, we're simply sitting in it. In 'just sitting' we're not expected to have a totally blank mind because that's like putting up a screen or barrier between ourselves and the world. Rather, we're working on quietening the ceaseless babble, suspending judgement, and simply being right where we are, mind and body wholly engaged in every moment of sitting. The lines about 'thinking' makes it sound more difficult than it needs to be:

Think about not thinking. What kind of thinking is not-thinking? Non-thinking.

Dogen takes this from a story about Master Yakuzan Igen and uses it to gently mock our intellectual angst. His instruction is achingly simple: just sit. But we can't leave it at that, we want more instruction. What should I think about when I'm sitting? The truth is we already know how to sit, we've done it for thousands of hours. How much thinking do we think it involves? We know zazen is a non-intellectual exercise and yet we want to know what we should be thinking about. Dogen ties us up in language knots and pushes us away. 'You want to know what to think about? Think about not thinking. How can you do that? It's a special method called non-thinking.'

Dogen is trying to stop the gap opening up – the gap between thinking and doing. For heaven's sake stop thinking about doing it and just get on with it. Every martial arts instructor in the world can relate to his frustration. How many hours do you have to waste with students and parents who want to know everything about karate: how and why and what and where and who – and yet they are usually the same people who spend the least amount of time in the dojo, doing the training. If they could shut the gap they would start to get the results they're so interested in.

Sitting in zazen is not Zen concentration. It is simply the dharma gate to joyful ease.

Dogen says it's not 'all in the mind'. It's more fundamental than that. This simple exercise is a gateway to seeing the world as it really is and enjoying the happiness that comes with it. This is uncharacteristically positive for Dogen. More often than not, he cautions us against expecting anything special from zazen. But here he says how great zazen can be. It is natural and wonderful. It makes us feel like a dragon returning to water (which, in China, is where dragons live) or a tiger returning to its home in the mountains. Like going back to where we belong.

Next he writes about the 'triggering' of awakening that is such an integral part of Zen tradition – a finger, a banner, a needle, or a mallet – and the bringing of realisation with a whisk, a fist, a staff, or a shout. These cannot be understood by discriminative thinking. They are real actions, or objects, that bring a student out of intellectual pondering and slap bang into reality. A punch in the face. A thwack with a stick. The whisk is a Buddhist symbol that a master would hold up to a student, as if to say 'This! This real object right in front of you'.

Dogen urges us again and again not to get hung up on irrelevancies but to do as the founders did and just sit. In karate it's the same. Just train. Warm up. Stretch. Punch. Kick. Practise kata. In doing this, we're doing as the masters did. In one sense, the same. Yet to the experienced eye, maybe differently and not so well. But each day better and a little closer to how the masters did things. Just as they did before.

Stop wasting time, Dogen says. Hurry up and get on with it because life is fleeting. It passes like a flash of lightning. In another chapter he tells us to train as if our heads were on fire. Then he uses a lovely metaphor from an old Zen story about a dragon, saying:

I beseech you, noble followers of Zen, do not become so accustomed to images of a mythical dragon that you are dismayed when you encounter a real one.

This comes from the story of a man who loved dragons and filled his home with pictures of them. But when a real dragon appeared outside his window, he was too afraid to look out. Dogen is warning us: don't let your idea of what something is stand in the way of seeing what it really is. This imagery appealed to Nishijima Roshi so much that he used it as the title for his book: To Meet the Real Dragon (which I highly recommend). Dogen ends by saying:

Devote your energies to the way of direct pointing at the truth. Revere those who have gone beyond learning and are free from effort. Accord with the enlightenment of the buddhas and become a rightful successor to the patriarchs. Live in such a way, and you will be such a person. The treasure store will open naturally and you will be able to enjoy it freely.

Live in such a way and you will be such a person. This is the crux of the matter. You are what you do. Not what you think, but what you do. No amount of wanting will ever achieve anything. But even the smallest amount of doing is a step in the right direction.

I saw a meme the other day that made me smile. I can't remember the exact wording but it had a picture of a runner and the headline said something like: The UK Running

Club's official guide to becoming a runner. Along the bottom it said: Go for a run.

Train like a Zen master and one day, you will become a Zen master. Train like a karate master and one day, you will become a karate master. Don't be under any illusion, that means a lot of training. So don't let thinking and wishing and dreaming and research and 'shopping around' get in the way of getting on with it. Just get on with it.

BALANCING BODY AND MIND

After a few weeks with the Dogen Sangha I was feeling more comfortable with both the people, who really were a great bunch, and the sitting. I'd learnt how to get the cushions set up right to achieve a firm base and my mind had calmed down from its initial roar of excitement. No longer was it like a Red Setter let off the leash in the park. Now it merely flitted around having nice thoughts pop along for a visit, like a series of polite house guests coming over for a chat. The guests were great company. They had great ideas for books, or useful insights into Zen and karate and it would have been rude to ask them to leave. More than once, I wished I could bring a notebook into the meditation hall. 'Would it bother anyone if I scribbled down some ideas in my Moleskine?'

This open-house policy was getting out of hand so I decided to try and close the door. I wanted to give myself something solid and firm to concentrate on. An image of a mountain came to mind. That's pretty solid. At first it was a real mountain and then it changed to a Japanese brush-stroke image of a mountain, just two simple lines that created Mount Fuji. The mountain was an easy image to concentrate on. The two lines of the slope pointed to the spot directly in front of me that was the peak. I knew that ultimately, in sitting, we're not supposed to concentrate on one thing, but I found it useful as a way to get my mind back under control. Useful, but ultimately, not right.

It occurred to me that zazen is different to karate in one important respect because no one knows how well you're doing, except you. Maybe not even you. Your teacher can't see what's going on (or not going on) in your head. Apart from adjusting your posture while you're sitting, they can't do much to help you.

(In later discussions with Mike, I was informed that this is not strictly true and he can see when someone is 'fully inhabiting what they are doing'. When he sees people sitting, it's clear to him whether they have fully embraced the practice or not. The parallels with karate were closer than I thought!)

But as a beginner, I wondered how do you measure progress? Should you even be measuring progress? And progress towards what? Dogen tells us not to aim to achieve anything from sitting. Just sit. Not having a goal feels very strange to a Western mindset.

I knew that in truth, my mind was all over the place. At first I told myself that I only had a minute or two of 'non-thinking' during my hour of sitting. Later, when I was being more honest with myself, I think it was more like a second or two.

It was time to leave the masterless thrashing of my mind alone for a while and learn a bit more about the other important aspect of Zen that's often ignored: the body.

After sitting, we read Nishijima Roshi's theories on the physical aspects of zazen. This was one of the great things about the group I'd joined. While we were referencing texts that were 800 years old, our teachers were able to integrate modern science into their understanding of Dogen. Best of all, there seemed to be no contradiction, science simply helped to explain better how things work – including zazen.

After many years of studying Western philosophy, psychology and physiology, Nishijima developed a theory of how sitting balances body and mind. Buddhism is often called the 'Middle Way' between extremes, for example between asceticism (denial) and materialism (excess), seeking to tone down the pull-push effects of cravings and aversions and find a middle ground. But when Nishijima investigated the body he found there are similar unconscious push-and-pull forces at work. The autonomic nervous system manages the functions of vital organs like the heart, lungs and digestion automatically. It is split into two parts, the sympathetic and parasympathetic systems that have contradictory functions.

The sympathetic nervous system arouses the body and stimulates 'fight or flight' responses. The heart-rate goes up to feed muscles for action. Pupils dilate to let in more light and help us see further. Digestion is put on hold and excess baggage is vacated from the bladder and bowels. Blood pumps away from the skin to feed the vital organs. In short, it stimulates you.

Meanwhile the parasympathetic nervous system says, 'Hang on second, there's no need to get all hot and bothered. Sit down and take a load off. The parasympathetic system is all about R&R. The heart rate slows. Pupils dilate. Digestion kicks back in and everyone takes a nice long out-breath.

The two systems work in opposition to one another, complementary rather than antagonistic. One useful description I found was to think of the sympathetic system as the accelerator and the parasympathetic system as the brake. When one is in operation, the other backs off.

But which system is working doesn't depend on you, or your brain, but rather the environment your body finds itself in. Faced with dangerous or stressful circumstances, the body gets aroused. Faced with a non-threatening environment, the body relaxes and replenishes.

If we think of our current lives, it's easy to see how the body is rarely in balance. The alarm clock rings and we stumble out of bed, stepping on a phone charger or a kid's toy. There's someone in the bathroom so we have to wait. We don't have time for breakfast, just coffee. The traffic is bad. The bus isn't moving. The train's delayed. There's a pile of crap in our inbox. The project is needed by tomorrow and half the team's off sick. Oh, and the boss wants a word. The sympathetic system is working overtime, just like us. We get home and hit the sofa. Hit the wine. Eat too much. Watch a few hours of mindless nonsense on the box. Now the parasympathetic system is in full flow, with lots of ground to make up. It's easy to see that too much of either isn't doing us any good. And this is what Nishijima is driving at. It's hard to think of many activities in our daily lives that achieve a good balance of activity and relaxation, where the mind isn't either flying off all over the place or totally zoning out. Or where the body is neither wholly active nor totally relaxed.

But zazen does this. The carefully structured posture aligns the vertebrae of the spine. These are rings made of bone surrounding the spinal cord. In between each vertebra are small muscles that we can't move consciously. These muscles get tense from sitting in stressful positions at desk and chairs and in meetings and the vertebrae can get pressed and squashed, so the nerves get pinched, affecting the signals they send to the vital organs. Sitting in zazen allows the muscles around the spine to soften, lengthen and settle. In my case it takes about fifteen minutes and I can literally feel it happening.

With the small muscles relaxed and a straight spine, the nerve signals are no longer interrupted and the body is in a nicely balanced state, mentally and physically.

I'd come to the group thinking Zen was a chance to delve deeper into the mental and spiritual aspects of karate, but I was beginning to realise it wasn't that simple. Mind and body are one. Neither can exist without the other. The body is fully involved in zazen, just as it is in a fight. The idea that we're made up of component parts like the brain, the nervous system, muscles and tendons, skin and bone can be a useful way of thinking about ourselves, but none of these divisions can exist apart in reality.

A PHILOSOPHY OF ACTION

Mind and body need to act in a unified whole to do karate properly. To move. To perform. To fight. This I could readily accept. I knew it to be true from my own experience. But I found another of Mike's assertions much more difficult to accept – namely that zazen was action.
Mike spoke often about how simple actions such as walking, climbing or swimming could bring about a similar effect to zazen – the absence of discriminatory thought, a kind of losing oneself in action. He gave many more examples, of which karate was one: playing musical instruments, moulding clay, painting, cooking. But when he included zazen in this group of activities, I found it hard to accept. Karate was action. Sitting stock still on a cushion was the opposite of action. It took a while for me to see that Mike was talking in very subtle terms rather than obvious, big movements. It was only when he went into some detail about 'sitting' that I found I could fully accept what he was saying.
The word 'sitting' is in the continuous present tense. This makes it an ongoing action. We are choosing to sit at each moment. We could get up any time we liked, but we are

continuing to sit. Moreover, we're not fixed and locked solid. While there may be little or no movement visible to the naked eye, the act of sitting upright on a cushion is an act of balancing. And just like balancing with one foot on a ball, balancing is an activity, not a fixed or completed action.

Mike showed how, in his own sitting, he would attend to his posture and balance by checking his body and making microscopic adjustment. Perfect balance doesn't exist in any permanent way. It is a concept. In reality we will always fall short. Nevertheless, it gives us something to aim for.

This was a bit of a turning point for me in my sitting. It freed me up to consider 'sitting' an action and allow myself a little movement in the spine and muscles, to gently keep myself on balance. It helped me to develop a key aspect of advanced martial arts, which is the self-awareness to go inside your own body and examine your muscular tensions and relaxations.

But is this 'just sitting'? Isn't checking your posture 'thinking' about your posture? Yes it is. Sitting is not one thing, locked down in mind or body. Sitting is an exercise that's surprisingly diverse, considering there's not a lot going on. Finding the right posture. Clearing the mind. Noticing a thought. Gently ushering it away. Rechecking the posture. Relaxing the jaw. Thinking about dinner. Coming back to sitting. Checking posture. Just sitting. Thinking about dinner. Noticing the sound of a rumbling stomach. Your stomach. Being a little bit embarrassed, but not too much. It's just a natural aspect of the human body and nothing to be ashamed of. Just the parasympathetic nervous system doing its job. Going back to just sitting. Adjusting posture. Thinking that at least you didn't fart, because that would have been embarrassing.

One of my favourite descriptions of zazen comes from the American Zen master Brad Warner, in his book 'Don't Be a Jerk'. He tells of a visit to a river in Germany where some concrete construction under the surface has created a standing wave. People come and surf this wave. They stay on for as long as they can, and then they fall off. Brad describes his sitting like this. He rides his non-thought for as long as he can before he crashes, and then gets right back on again.

The subtle action of sitting in a balanced posture and staying present in what we're doing right now is a useful practice in any situation. And if there's an example to follow, that always helps.

THE BUDDHA

Zen traces its origins to Gautama Buddha, a prince, born to a noble clan in northern India in what is now Nepal. The exact dates of his birth and death aren't certain. Earlier scholars put it around 500BC but more recently it's believed to be closer to 400BC.

The word 'Buddha' isn't a name, it simply means someone who is awake. A person who sees reality as it truly is. In

Buddhist tradition, we all have the possibility to awaken to reality and there have been many buddhas in history. Gautama Buddha is revered as *The Buddha* because he established a practice that continues to this day, enabling followers to shed delusion and awaken to reality.

According to Buddhist history, the young Gautama grew up in luxury, sheltered from normal life inside a guarded compound. But when he went outside the gate, he saw sickness, old age and death. Even today in India, these things aren't hidden from view, as they often are in the West. They are right there in front of you.

He saw suffering all around and wanted to find a way to alleviate the pain of everyday life. He felt the religions of the day didn't have the answer. In the end, he gave up his inheritance and left his family to go in search of the truth.

He visited the religious leaders of the time but couldn't find what he was looking for. He spent years with yogis and hermits in the forest, trying all sorts of ascetic practices and nearly starved to death. Eventually, he realised that while self-denial has some virtues, it wasn't getting him any closer to the real truth. In this famished state the mind played tricks on him but this wasn't the same as seeing reality.

In one of his key decisions, which became his first sermon, he decided to adopt a 'Middle Way' and started eating again. The 'Middle Way' is a very important concept of Buddhism. It sounds like a bit of a compromise but in reality it is anything but – as Gudo Nishijima explains:

When we can see two sides clearly, the middle ground also becomes visible. Buddhism occupies this middle ground. But the middle way is not a compromise. It is a clear choice, a clear alternative. To walk in the middle way is to reject the extremes and enter the real world.

The Middle Way is not an easy way. It's far less bother to adopt an extreme, clear-cut view, because that way you don't have to think. You just obey the rules, the law, word for word. Black is black. White is white. It's far more troublesome to accept that nothing is ever this simple. We need to be prepared, at all times, to see every viewpoint. Not necessarily to agree with it, but to see it and hear it. Not because it's nice or fair or palatable, but because it exists. So it is real.

After this, Gautama Buddha decided to go it alone. He sat for weeks under a giant fig tree before finally, one night, awakening to reality. His awakening revealed the following, which became his fundamental teachings, summarised as the Four Noble Truths:

1. Life is characterised by suffering
2. The cause of suffering is desire
3. Only eradicating desire can eradicate suffering
4. To eradicate desire, follow the Eightfold Path

The Four Noble Truths might sound a bit simple. Yes, there is suffering in the world, no one is denying that. But there is also joy and kindness, sometimes, if you look hard enough. The suffering the Buddha meant isn't all suffering, but rather unnecessary suffering – the kind we bring on ourselves. Which, in truth, is an awful lot. This can be as simple as our own desires and cravings that aren't good for us and lead to unhappiness. Or fears and aversions that prevent us from acting correctly. But they can also be things we do that harm others. On a global scale, the greed of one dictator is enough to launch a whole country into war, which leads to a whole lot more suffering.

But the Buddha's teachings are aimed squarely at the individual first. Let's get our own house into order before we look at others. How do we do this? By eradicating desire. All desire? What if you're hungry and desire a plate of food?

The desires we're talking about are unhealthy desires, cravings and longings that don't do us, or anyone else, any good. How do we rid ourselves of these unnatural cravings? The Fourth Noble Truth leads us neatly onto a set of guidelines called the Eightfold Path:

1. Right view
2. Right thought
3. Right speech
4. Right action
5. Right livelihood
6. Right effort
7. Right mindfulness
8. Right concentration

This is a simple framework designed to help us act correctly and get along. But it's important to realise that what's 'right' in each case remains deliberately undefined. There is no such thing as 'Right' that exists outside an action itself. Right means right at the time. Right in the circumstances. This avoids us getting locked into rigid rules that prevent us from acting correctly in the moment.

Right View is first because it means seeing things clearly, just as they are, unhindered by preconceived ideas. If we can't do this, nothing else will follow. This is a very difficult first hurdle. We often have a kind of natural denial that anything bad or wrong has anything to do with us. It must be someone else's fault. 'They' are to blame.

Right View is difficult because admitting our own faults means the ego takes a battering. A fragile ego will do an awful lot to avoid getting bruised, inventing all sorts of reasons why we can't do this, that, or the other. Why someone else is to blame. In the martial arts this is often our teacher, our style, the other students. At home it might be our parents, our partner, the husband, the wife, the kids. At work it's the customer, the client, the boss. Anyone but ourselves. This is the sort of thing we can often see quite clearly in others, and they in turn can see it in us. But can we see it in ourselves?

Even admitting to the possibility of our own involvement is a huge step in the right direction. Once we have the confidence to truly analyse our own actions and motives, seeing clearly becomes easier. And everything else starts to follow. Good things start to happen.

Right Thought, Right Speech and Right Action are just as they suggest. Once you can see a situation as it really is, you can consider it properly and make better decisions – Right Thought. You can talk honestly and truthfully – Right Speech. You can act appropriately – Right Action. You can 'think', 'say' and 'do' the right thing.

Point 5, 'Right Livelihood,' means it's hard to do the right thing if your work involves doing the wrong thing. Traditionally, this would be things that cause suffering to humans or animals, like trading in living beings (slavery), weapons, meat, alcohol or poison. Today, it might be being a personal injury lawyer. Basically, if you find it hard to look at yourself in the mirror, then it might be worth changing jobs. Or careers.

Right Effort, Right Mindfulness and Right Concentration help us keep to the previous guidelines. To continue seeing, thinking, speaking and acting correctly, we need to maintain a constant effort. Right Effort. We need to remain aware of these things. Right Mindfulness. The final step on the Eightfold Path, Right Concentration, means keeping the mind clear, focused and aware, day to day, moment to moment. How do we manage this difficult task? The answer is Dogen's answer to pretty much everything: zazen.

The importance of regular meditation is repeated by every Zen master you'll meet, and in every Zen book you'll read. With the emphasis on regular. It doesn't need to be hours on end. Most suggest an hour a day, split between morning and evening. All night sessions may sound super-extreme for iron monks on mist covered mountains, but for everyday folk just a little daily discipline is the key. And anything is better than nothing.

The same is certainly true in karate. Extreme training can be challenging, rewarding and inspiring, but it's the daily routine that builds real progress – the 'slow gains' that accumulate, layer by layer, over time, bringing improvement so slowly you can't even feel it. Like walking in mist, as Dogen puts it – you don't notice you're getting wet, but you end up soaked through.

What do you make of the Eightfold Path? It seems to be a fairly simple set of guidelines, not dissimilar to what the Bible lists as the Seven Deadly Sins – not much more than a Sunday School collection of do's and don'ts. The kind of thing you knew already, and hardly the revelatory thinking you'd expect from someone as remarkable as The Buddha. In Dogen's bible, the Shobogenzo, there's a chapter titled, 'Not Doing Wrong'.

A famous poet asks his master, 'What is the great intention of the Buddha's teachings?'

The master replies, 'Not doing wrong. Doing right.'

The poet's a bit disappointed by such a simple answer and complains that even a three-year-old child can say this.

The master says, 'A child of three can say it, but an old man of eighty can't do it.'

We know what we should do. It's so simple, even a child knows it. But there are so many reasons why we can't, shouldn't, mustn't, wouldn't, couldn't... so many that we could spend a lifetime trying and failing to act correctly.

We know the Eightfold Path makes sense. It's a way to treat everyone, including ourselves, with care and compassion and good old Buddhist loving-kindness. We know from experience that it's right. If we're mean to our brothers and sisters, they're mean to us. If we harm others, they harm us. If we tell lies, it leads to more lies, and more trouble. We know these things make us unhappy. And most of us have some of it under control. But how do we get it all under control? Or even better, how do we stop it coming up in the first place? This is where zazen really kicks in, quietening the mind and showing us how our own thought processes work. Giving us time to settle down and not say or do the first ugly thing that pops into our heads.

In my own experience, since I've begun meditating seriously, I've felt more prepared to face the world. Even a short period in the morning sets me up nicely for the day. It's hard to put my finger on exactly what it does for me. The general consensus at the Dogen Sangha is that it's much easier to notice the effect of zazen when you don't sit. You miss that subtle, settled feeling. It's not an ongoing state, it's a daily thing. A few minutes lasts a few hours. Keeping it small and regular seems to be the key.

After the Buddha's death, it was another 400 years before his teaching came to be written down. By this point they had spread far and wide, from the Ganges region in northern India, south as far as Sri Lanka, east into Burma, Thailand and Southeast Asia, and north into modern day Pakistan, Afghanistan and the so-called Russian 'Stans' of Central Asia.

Each strand of Buddhism came to emphasise different things. The Central Asian strand eventually spread along the trade routes known as the Silk Road into China. This branch was known as Mahayana and it concentrated on the Buddha's awakening to reality. And it was Mahayana Buddhism that was taught by the first patriarch of Zen, and the legendary founder of Shaolin martial arts. A monk who may or may not have existed, but either way, who left an indelible impression on the culture of the Far East and by extension, the world.

BODHIDHARMA

By the time Bodhidharma was teaching in Shaolin, around 520AD, Buddhism was already well established in China. There were thousands of Buddhist temples in both the northern and southern dynasties that ruled a divided empire. But while other schools were concentrating on scriptures, ceremonies and good deeds (and saying it could take a lifetime to reach enlightenment and maybe even longer) Bodhidharma was saying something radically different. Enlightenment could be instantaneous. It was within the grasp of each of us in every moment. In the words of his modern-day biographer, Red Pine:

While others viewed Zen as purification of the mind or a stage on the way to buddhahood, Bodhidharma equated Zen with buddhahood – and buddhahood with everyday mind. Instead of telling his disciples to purify their minds, he pointed them to rock walls, to the movements of tigers and cranes, to a hollow reed floating across the Yangtze, to a single sandal.

Whether Bodhidharma was a real person is debatable. Personally, I'm very fond of him and what he stands for – so fond that I wrote a novel about him – but I'm happy to accept that instead of Bodhidharma (the man) teaching at Shaolin, Bodhi-Dharma (which means 'Awakening Teachings') were *being taught* at Shaolin.

The earliest accounts of Bodhidharma are very sketchy. The first mention of him at Shaolin was written over a hundred years later, and his story got embellished further as time went on. Much of what is written is clearly allegorical and designed to make a point, to educate and inspire, rather than represent a fully accurate account. All accounts agree he came from the West, most likely India, but possibly Central Asia or even Persia. He's said to have had blue eyes and a red beard, probably to emphasis his 'barbarian' (non-Chinese) origins. His family background is similar to the Buddha's. He was the son of a nobleman, born to a high caste, either a Brahmin (priest) or Kshatriya (warrior). Like the Buddha, he gave up a rich and noble life to follow the Way and he made the dangerous journey to China as a missionary to spread the Buddha-Dharma.

Most accounts have Bodhidharma arriving by sea in the south and visiting the emperor Wu Di in the southern capital, Nanjing. His interview with the emperor is said to have gone something like this: The emperor asked who he was and Bodhidharma said he didn't know. The emperor asked what he taught and Bodhidharma replied, 'Vast emptiness, nothing sacred'. The emperor asked how much merit he (the emperor) had acquired for his support of Buddhism and Bodhidharma answered, 'No merit'.

If he was hoping for imperial patronage, Bodhidharma's interview technique clearly needed some work. But if we consider the allegory behind the exchange, we can unpick the intended lessons. Bodhidharma's answers highlight the key aspects of Mahayana Buddhism and the differences with the other Buddhist sects at the time.

'Not knowing' is shorthand for not being caught up in a conceptual view of reality. The idea of not knowing his own name, or who he was, is what Dogen calls 'forgetting the self'. Losing the sense we have of ourselves as separate from the world around us. To let, as Dogen puts it, 'body and mind fall away'.

Teaching 'Vast emptiness, nothing sacred,' is a reference to Sunyata – usually translated as 'emptiness'. In this case, emptiness doesn't mean nothingness or a void, but rather that nothing is fixed or permanent. Everything is transitory. To think of anything as permanent, including ourselves, is to be deluded. A thing is only a thing in the moment. By the next moment, it is something else. It has changed, maybe very slightly, but it has changed. So if we want to be totally and utterly correct about the form a thing takes, we must say it has no lasting and abiding form. It is empty of form.

This is a vital aspect of Zen and one that you might have heard before. But it pays to really think about it and get to grips with it. Look at a photo of yourself as a child. Or even five years ago. Who is this person? We call it 'me' or 'I' but that self keeps changing. In reality, there is no fixed and permanent 'I' – only the idea of yourself that you carry with you, moment by moment.

The concept of Emptiness is important, but it's not sacred. Bodhidharma isn't offering a fixed doctrine but simply pointing to the truth – something each of us can see any time, if we let go of our preconceptions.

He refuses to flatter the emperor and pander to his ego, or 'self'. The emperor has amassed no merit for all his good deeds. This answer is another change from traditional Buddhism where doing good deeds builds up good karma and a favourable rebirth. In Zen, the whole idea of building up credits (known as merit) is considered just another form of attachment to Samsara – the wheel of life that's characterised by suffering.

Bodhidharma's answers show the stark truth of his Buddhism – so stark, he won't play ball, not even with an emperor. This uncompromising honesty is rarely popular and unsurprisingly, it didn't go down well with the emperor. Bodhidharma left with no imperial patronage and went to visit the northern Wei dynasty, where he ended up at Shaolin. Here, it is said, he sat in a cave and gazed at the wall so intently that his eyes bored holes in the rock. His legs withered and fell off and he cut off his own eyelids to prevent himself from falling asleep. These descriptions are caricatures intended to stress the importance of zazen. Meditation had always been a part of Buddhism, but Bodhidharma made it the bedrock of his practice.

His successor, Hui Ko, asked him to pacify his mind. Bodhidharma told Hui Ko to bring him his mind and he would pacify it. This helped Hui Ko to realise that in reality, there was no such thing as his mind that exists outside himself. It was inseparable from his body, which was inseparable from the air and the world around him. Once he realised this, Ko's agitation subsided. Bodhidharma had snapped him out of his self-induced problem, out of the realm of thought and into reality.

Later, when he was preparing to leave, Bodhidharma gathered four of his disciples and asked what each of them had learnt. The first said, 'The Way is not found in scriptures, nor is it outside scriptures.' Bodhidharma said, 'You have got my skin.' The second said, 'My understanding now is like seeing the Buddha-land once and never again.' Bodhidharma said, 'You have attained my flesh.' The third said, 'The four elements are empty, the five senses are misleading, there's not a single thing to be attained.' Bodhidharma said, 'You have my bones.' The last of the four, Hui Ko, remained silent and Bodhidharma said, 'You have my marrow.' Each of the four answers satisfied Bodhidharma, and each said, in some way, that the teachings must be abandoned before Bodhidharma's essence can be attained. The first said it most clearly. The way is not found in scriptures, nor is it outside scriptures. Scriptures point to the way, but they are not the actual way.

Nevertheless, the pointing is accurate and therefore useful. The second said once the benefit of the teachings has been attained, there's no need to keep going over them. Once we see the 'Buddha Land' there is no need to keep revisiting it. Bodhidharma liked this answer too, perhaps more than the first, since it reached deeper than his skin, into his flesh. The third answer said everything, even the idea of attaining enlightenment and nirvana, is empty. These things don't exist in the way we imagine them. Bodhidharma liked this answer best of all... so far. It reached to his bones.

Finally, the fourth disciple, Hui Ko, said nothing at all. He'd gone beyond the need for words and explanations. He just 'got it'. His once-troubled mind had finally been pacified. Now he knew his own mind and no longer needed a master to affirm it.

This seemed to satisfy Bodhidharma best of all. He passed on his robe and bowl to Hui Ko and made him his successor. Hui Ko's understanding penetrated all the way to the core. To the marrow – a depth of understanding that requires no words. An acknowledgement that words can never capture the whole truth.

Centuries later, the idea of marrow returned in a more physical form, as part of Bodhidharma's so-called Eighteen Bone Marrow Cleansing exercises. This was just one of a series of physical practices attributed to him.

Bodhidharma was probably Indian and almost certainly familiar with yoga, which he would have taught to help his disciples sit for long hours in the lotus position. That these were martial exercises is, in truth, unlikely. The evidence at the Shaolin Temple shows the monks engaged in battles around a hundred years later, but there is no mention of their using their own techniques or methods. The modern Shaolin historian Meir Shahar makes a convincing argument that the monks developed armed and unarmed combat methods much later in the Ming dynasty (1368 – 1644) and these became popularised later still in 20th century literature.

Bodhidharma marked a new and distinct direction in Buddhism, a particular flavour that would evolve to become Zen and influence a huge array of martial arts around the world. He changed enlightenment from something faraway and distant and wonderful to something simple and real and attainable at any moment – if only we could stop wishing for it and start doing something more practical instead.

There's a great deal written about enlightenment, the awakening of the 'Buddha Mind'. To awaken to reality is often considered the purpose of zazen. To reach nirvana. However there is much debate and argument, even among Zen schools, as to how this happens. Some contend that it happens gradually with small steps towards enlightenment. Others have a different view, saying it happens all at once and can occur at any moment. Others still choose not to focus on achieving the Buddha state any time soon and probably not in this lifetime. Just follow the Buddhist path of right thought and right action for the benefit of all sentient beings.

As a relative newcomer to Zen, I won't comment on

enlightenment and awakening in Buddhist practice. All I can offer is my own experience in karate and for me, all three versions are, in some way, true. And not one wholly captures how these things really work.

SUDDEN AWAKENING

In truth, every moment you train is an opportunity to make progress. Every bow, every punch, every push-up and sit-up is a chance to improve and deepen your practice. The trouble is you're often unaware of the improvement and feel very little is happening. That's because each time you get a bit better, you train a bit harder, so it never feels any easier. This 'unfelt progress' doesn't become apparent until you see a fresh batch of beginners struggling to do what you can do now without too much trouble.

If you stick with the training, week in, week out, adding an extra day here and there, getting more serious, you will one day get your green belt, and your brown belt, and your black belt. In one sense you have achieved something wonderful. In another you're still no better off. You're so much stronger and better, but the level expected of you is so much higher that it's still not easy.

While this step-by-step method brings steady progress, every once in a while there are moments when something big happens. The rewards of a long period of hard training get dumped on you all at once. These can be moments of revelation, when something you couldn't comprehend suddenly becomes clear. Or simple 'doh!' moments when you can't believe you've been so stupid for so long. Or moments of what I'd call 'spiritual progress', when you face a big fear and come out the other side, resetting your self-imposed boundaries by a considerable way. My first full-contact fight was a good example of this. It was a huge stepping stone for me. Until that time, I'd only engaged in sparring, sometimes light and friendly, sometimes hard and brutal, but never with the intent of knocking someone out – or someone knocking me out.

The knockdown tournament was a whole new ball game because the intention was different. Beforehand I suffered from some nerves (although not too badly because I'd prepared well) and in my first fight I went toe-to-toe with a top competitor and a knockout specialist. To my surprise, I was doing rather well, until I lost concentration and got winded. But even though I lost, I gained so much from the experience. From that day to this, sparring has been easier thanks to those two short minutes of fighting. It's hard to get anxious when you know you can handle a whole lot more. This test gave me the emotional freedom to relax and enjoy my sparring for years to come.

My biggest moment of revelation came in the run-up to my third dan grading. Knowing that I would be tested on every detail of every stance and block and punch, I spent hours going in-depth on each technique. And after a few days, I noticed something profoundly different in my karate. Instead of doing a facsimile of what my instructor had been asking for, I was actually doing it as I was supposed to do.

And the results were remarkable. My kicks and punches seemed to flow with natural power. There was a feeling that I wasn't having to make all the effort any more. Nature was helping. Gravity was helping. Momentum was helping. I was somehow connected with natural forces and able to channel them.

This isn't as special as it sounds. It's simply 'body mechanics' at work, the correct use of physics that makes everything easier, so you get more power with less effort. However the real revelation, which came much later, was that in some way, I'd known this all along. My instructors had been telling me to do things this way from day one. I'd listened, but not really heard. This knowledge and ability had been available to me for fifteen years before I began to make real use of it.

After my initial surprise and excitement I felt annoyed, mainly with myself, that I'd taken so long to get it. I began trying to tell other people about it, other students, and pass it on a bit quicker. But after another while I realised you can't hurry this process. While the route to good karate is right in front of us, we can't find it. Moving in straight lines. Turning in smooth circles. It sounds so simple but it takes years to attain this simplicity.

If my first big enlightenment moment was emotional (believing in myself) and my second was physical (moving correctly), the final element was mental, and it took a good bit longer. Learning how to think in karate – how to think just about what you're doing, not analysing or over-thinking, not going into automatic and mindlessly 'under-thinking' but achieving the kind of 'just-right thinking' that's needed.

Towards the end of my fighting career, when I fought in tournaments, I'd matured as a fighter and I was far more technically proficient. I won a few fights fairly quickly. But in an important fight against one of the top competitors, I tried an elaborate tactic and got caught by a simple front-kick before I could pull it off. It was a good example of over-thinking.

The next year, I was able to keep my mind 'just-so' and scored point after point with no overthinking getting in the way. I was able to focus on hitting targets and nothing else. Actually, that's not true. While scoring was my goal, I paid a small regard to my opponent's strikes, just enough to avoid them, before landing my own. This is a delicate balance that you have to maintain.

The weight of the balance needs to be in favour of the goal – striking, and a smaller amount (as little as possible) needs to be weighted towards not being struck. I managed to get the balance right and with no other thoughts or ideas or strategies or doubts popping up to ruin things, I took the gold medal in short order. And I won the grappling section too, which I wasn't expecting. However the learning from tournaments wasn't the same as the learning from my biggest martial arts test, the 30 Man Kumite. I have written about this experience in depth elsewhere, but in case you haven't read those highly absorbing accounts, I'll summarise as follows: one person fights a line-up of 30 of the highest grades in the association. Each round lasts one minute and as soon as one finishes, the next begins. All fights are full-contact and there are just two short breaks after ten and twenty fights.

In this event, you are pushed to your limit early, and then held there for a very long time. It doesn't take much more than five fights to make you tired. After this, it's a question of hanging on and fighting as best you can. In my test, my mind wavered and lurched in several directions. At first I was over-confident. But when I saw someone fail in the line ahead of me, it shook my confidence badly and for a long time all I wanted to do was survive. It wasn't until the last ten fights that I realised I was going to complete the task and I felt a bit more fight in me. Finally my mind settled and I finished the hardest part of the test in good form and without too much bother. This was a huge learning experience for me and afterwards I found it easier to keep my mind on the job.

In the last few tournaments of my career, I recall having no real nerves, just a good level of excitement that's needed to fight. I found my mind, body and spirit worked together as a team.

There are two fights that I recall most vividly. The first was against Dave Urquhart, a very tall, fast fighter who'd won the tournament consistently over the years. Even so, I felt no serious worry or doubt. I was confident in my ability and I planned to win. I knew about his lightning fast front kick and straight punches, his whipping round kick that explodes on the ribs. I was ready to keep out of his range and wait for a moment to enter his space. Usually that moment is just after one of his kicks, when his bodyweight is committed and he can't fire another shot (yet). My plan worked. I was getting into his space, catching him with some good straight punches. But Dave's plan was working too. He was catching me with kicks, and, when I came in close, knee strikes. After one round of furious action the referees called a break and conferred on points. They told us the scores were very close. We fought again. I held to my strategy because it was working, at least some of the time, and I couldn't think of a better one. At the end of the second bout the decision was called… and Dave won. I'd suspected he had, although I'd been fighting to win all the way to the bell.

Half an hour later, with the withdrawal of another competitor through injury, I had the chance to get back into the tournament. And guess who I would be fighting? Dave. I'd lost before. But that was before. I considered changing my strategy, since it hadn't resulted in a win. What could I do different? Trying to turn it into a war and bully him wouldn't work. Dave was far bigger than me and I knew I was better off keeping things civil. Rushing in and fighting from the clinch was another possibility, but Dave was strong, with vicious knees and good sweeps. I decided I had the most chance of winning by sticking to my original strategy and punishing his mistakes.

I stepped onto the mat and bowed, confident I was going to win. I would use slip timing, enter in off his techniques, and this time I would catch him. We fought for one blistering minute and again, it was close. We went another round and Dave wasn't giving anything away. At the end the refs conferred. We bowed and the decision went Dave's way again, by a close decision. Dave hadn't made any mistakes. If he had, I'd have won. But he hadn't.

Rather than regretting losing, I took away something positive about my performance in both fights. I'd fought with confidence. I'd remained positive. I'd stayed in the moment. I'd had a strategy and tactics and I'd stuck to them. I hadn't made mistakes, or had wobbles, or doubts, or fears. I'd been every bit as good as I could be. My only problem had been that Dave was just a little bit better.

ED AND LAILA

One of my key roles in the karate club is acting as an unofficial coach for fighters who have signed up for the gruelling 30 Man Kumite. It's something I learn from each time, because every person is different. Each new fighter is a new challenge to get up to scratch and see how far they can go.

This year I had an unlikely pair, Ed and Laila, who, on paper, seemed poles apart. When I'd met Laila at London's City University she'd been training in fencing. I'd been teaching a karate class and we were using the sports hall after her. I'd been told we could start at 7pm but when we tried to set up, the fencers seemed to think they had the hall until 7.30. With a little checking I was proved right – which surprised me as much as anyone – and the fencers packed up, albeit a bit slowly and reluctantly. While we were putting the mats down, one young fencer asked what we were doing and I told her Goju Ryu karate. She told me she had an orange belt in another style and asked if she could try our class. I said she was welcome.

Laila turned out to be fit and determined from the start, and seemed fascinated to learn all about this new style of karate. Next week, when I turned up at seven, Laila spotted me in the doorway and yelled at the fencers to pack up and get out. They cleared the hall in double quick time and Laila trained with us again.

Unsurprisingly, she quit fencing soon after and threw herself into karate. She was young and fit but it was her ferocity that really shone out. She would attack the training and the exercises and her opponents with equal delight. In sparring she would buzz in and out with fast little steps and fighting her felt like being pecked by a swarm of angry sparrows. Her tenacity meant she went up through the grades with steady progress and soon her strikes were carrying more weight. The little birds had grown bigger, with sharp beaks and talons. She seemed to have tireless cardio and was able to dash in and out for the whole class without ever slowing down. Her only real weakness was balance, and every so often she would trip over her own feet, which was hardly surprising because they were moving so fast.

Laila made a big impression from day one and never looked back. Around the same time, another new face appeared and seemed to slip into the dojo with barely a whisper. I was vaguely aware of a new guy who'd come from a different style and wanted to try Goju Ryu. I had no idea of his name. Apparently he'd read Gavin's book, Four Shades of Black, and decided to join as a result. He was medium height but light and skinny, and around forty years old. The style he'd come from had some connection to Goju Ryu, but it was non-contact and ours was full-contact. Our club was filled with big guys and heavy hitters, so I didn't hold out much hope for him lasting.

He disappeared off my radar. But every so often, I'd see him with a new belt. Even though he'd been graded to purple belt in his old style, he'd started again at white belt. I don't remember seeing him get his red belt, or his yellow belt. Or orange. But by the time he'd got his green belt and the coveted DKK badge, I began to remember his name.

Ed's karate was good, but nothing special. Just normal. And yet his age had given him something that can be even more valuable than youth – maturity. Ed trained regularly and consistently. The fact that he was quiet meant he listened. He did every task put before him as best he could. And when you have this approach, nothing is beyond you. Some years later, both Ed and Laila were set to test for black belt. They teamed up with four others who were also grading and the six of them met every Saturday for months in advance. They drilled every aspect of the test and built their fitness week after week. Naturally with an attitude like this, all six nailed the grading in fine style and set an example for others to follow.

One moment from the grading sticks in my memory.

Somewhere near the end, after several hours of karate and some extreme 'beastings' around the field, a group of brown and black belt candidates were punching Thai pads. They'd been going for quite some time and even the youngest and strongest were tired and drooping. But one figure among them suddenly found some new energy and began punching with a savagery that belied the work he'd done before. His shoulders seemed to bulge and his arms were ripped and for a moment I wasn't sure who it was. Then I recognised Ed. Far from keeping up with the youngsters, he was leading the way.

Two years later, Ed and Laila were ready for their 2nd dan black belt grading and the 30 Man Kumite. Due to the severity of the test, candidates are required to actively request it, so there can be no question of their motivation. In checking the calendar and doing the sums, we worked out Ed would be fifty by the time of the test.

Did he really want it? I spoke with him to make sure. He was well aware of the dangers. He'd fought in plenty of 30 Man line-ups and knew how it would be. Ed thought about it for a week and then went ahead with the request. Laila did the same and Sensei Gavin agreed to both. I offered to help them to prepare and they both accepted.

In my experience of the 30 Man Kumite, one thing above all else is needed to get through in decent shape, and that's what I can best describe as 'staying in the game'. The fighters who performed well remained focused from beginning to end. Those who struggled 'looked away' at some point. Like so many things, staying focused is easy to say, hard to do. When you're tired and hurting, it's natural to start looking around and searching for a way out. But to pass the 30 Man test there is no other way than to keep fighting. If you start looking away, you'll be easier to hit. You'll take more strikes, and harder shots. Worst of all, you won't see them coming, so you won't be prepared.

Staying in the game, come hell or high water, takes mental strength. I knew both candidates had it but even so, for Ed, I was worried. He was light and skinny and turning fifty. Laila, I wasn't too worried about. I knew she would attack her training like she attacked everything else, with a cheerful aggression that makes light of hard work.

Both had the mindset to succeed. But technically, both had room for improvement. Laila needed to tone down her relentless footwork to a more measured pace and change her rapid-fire combinations to fewer shots with more power. Most of all, she needed to get her balance under control and stop tripping over her own feet. Without balance, you can't root into a punch and make it truly powerful.

On our first training session I was impressed with Ed's cardio. He'd been doing 400m sprints with his work-mates just for fun. Having done these myself, I knew what a killer they can be and they certainly weren't my idea of fun. This was good news, because Ed's fitness was high, so we could concentrate on other aspects of his training. Technically, Ed's posture was off and it made him a bit unbalanced and vulnerable. I wanted to put this right as soon as possible.

Each week, I would set the two of them a new task and

expect to see some improvement in the next session. With Laila it was always clear that she'd tried hard and the results were obvious. As for Ed, he would improve too. But Laila seemed to be pushing the pace and Ed often struggled to keep up. At times she seemed to be so far ahead of him that I worried about his confidence, but Ed did what he always did. He quietly got on with it and improved at his own pace.

One Sunday, Laila wasn't there and I trained alone with Ed. We worked on a drill designed to anticipate an opponent's kicks. We'd already drilled responses to four kicks in a sequence. But now I threw the kicks in a random order to see how many Ed could anticipate correctly. From past experience, I knew a well-tuned fighter will predict around eight out of ten correctly. Ed managed this, fortunately for him.

The next week, Laila trained alone with me and we tried the same routine. She was every bit as good as Ed – until I told her that Ed had managed eight out of ten. As soon as she heard this, she began missing kicks and getting frustrated. I realised I was to blame. She'd been reacting with a clear, unconcerned mind and doing fine. My comment had taken her out of this 'empty' state of 'Mushin' – no-mind – and added a new component: the issue of doing as well as, or better than, Ed.

Now you could argue that this added pressure is important because the test is performed under pressure. People are watching and shouting and screaming from the side-lines. The kicks are full-power, so they hurt if they land. And she would be far more tired than she was in training. But this exercise was all about reading the opponent – a fundamental skill that requires an open mind with no preconceptions or clutter. The reaction must be instant and this 'open-mind' takes time to achieve. I'd made that difficult for her by planting that little Ed-bomb, and I felt a tad guilty.

As the big day approached, Laila continued to improve, hitting far harder and moving more precisely, with only the occasional stutter. Meanwhile Ed got stronger and fitter but his posture continued to worry me. He was still leaning forward and leaving his chin exposed. No matter what I tried, I couldn't get him to break the habit. I spent some time at home thinking of the best exercise for him. In the end, I devised a shadow-boxing drill that made it very difficult to lean and I asked Ed to practice it over the next week. Then I waited and hoped to see some improvement. Time was getting short. There were just three weeks to go before the test. I was very pleased with Laila but still concerned about Ed. I had to face it that both were probably as good as they were going to get. Nevertheless, I wanted to give them one more experience, designed to test, and hopefully consolidate, their mindset. It was time for what I liked to call 'Psyche Week'.

One of the most difficult things to come to terms with during the 30 Man test is the feeling that none of your training is working. The line-up is simply too good and too strong. No matter who you are, no matter how fit, you don't get things your own way. When you feel your power and energy slipping away and evaporating – frighteningly fast – it's important to carry on regardless, rather than mentally stopping to wonder what went wrong.

So before this particular session, I explained Psyche Week and how it worked. Once we began, I would give them no encouragement, just criticism, pointing out everything they were doing wrong and generally making them feel like shit. I made it clear that this was just an exercise. Their job was to ignore the negativity and carry on like any other week. They were training to generate their own encouragement. I think it's a great exercise, but not everyone agrees! I asked if they wanted to try it, because it was optional and both agreed, although Laila seemed less certain than Ed.

Once we began, it was Laila who seemed to falter. When I was critical, there was a noticeable dip in her performance. She wasn't striking with her usual relish. Perhaps she wasn't as confident as she always appeared. The big surprise was Ed. My criticisms didn't seem to make any difference and he was content to blast the pads as hard as he could. Better still, I noticed a considerable change since last week. Ed was hitting and moving very naturally with no trace of the dreaded lean. I eased off on criticising Laila but went harder on Ed. He just continued, round after round, slamming the pad with punches and kicks that seemed to be coming from a much bigger guy. In the end I threw the pad down in annoyance.

'Dammit Ed!' I said, 'you're ruining the exercise'.

Ed looked puzzled.

'I can't fault you,' I complained. Ed's weeks and months of quiet dedication had finally paid off, just in time for the big test. He deserved this moment and I was truly happy to share it with him. He was happy too, because until then, I'd always had some problem or other and now he'd finally managed to shut me up.

I spoke with Laila and reassured her that her performance had been fine. She'd succeeded in shutting out most of the negativity. This had been an exercise like any other – something we can all get better at if we try. But how do we achieve these changes in mentality? We can't simply tell ourselves to think different. Thinking is just thinking. Words are just words. How do we dig deep and change our behaviour? We start small, by acting differently just for one moment. *This* moment. One small moment of reality. Then we can begin to extend it. Change takes time and happens gradually. Changes in deep-down thinking, in behaviour and outlook, come through cultivating this approach little and often, day by day, hour by hour, minute by minute. As Dogen says, 'Live in such a way, and you will be such a person.'

Ed and Laila's preparation was complete. Their training and approach had been exemplary and all that remained was the test itself. I knew Laila would pass. The only question was whether she would shine as brightly as she was capable of doing. As for Ed, I felt more confident now. But 30 hard fights at 50 years of age would be a hell of a test and I was far from sure. Then again, what did I know? Because as it happened, nothing at all went as expected.

NO RETREAT

It was time to up my Zen training. Until this point, I'd only attended evening sittings rather than the longer retreats, known as 'Sesshin'. But now, I'd signed up for a three-day Sesshin in Scotland. The flight was booked and there was no going back. The thought of sitting for almost six hours a day, three days in a row, concerned me. I knew I needed to train for it and the best way would be to attend one of the day-retreats held, not in the Highlands but a little closer to home, in a community hall in Angel.

As I rang the security buzzer outside the gate, even this concerned me. It would be three hours of sitting instead of the usual one and I wondered how well I'd manage. I'd brought my own cushion and managed to get comfortable. The first hour went quickly and afterwards, Mike spoke about a TV series called 'The Brain.' I'd been watching it avidly. It was fascinating and, I felt, full of important matters relating to Zen and karate and the nature of consciousness. Things like: what makes you 'you'? And even the so called 'muscle-memory' that's so important in martial arts.

Just the week before, I'd watched an episode featuring a free-climber, hanging by his fingertips above a spectacular fall. The climber spoke of how he entered what he called the 'flow-state' that meant he did nothing but climb. Watching him hanging by one hand while his other hand sought a tiny finger-hold somewhere above, it was clear any rational consideration of his situation would have been deeply unhelpful, and potentially lethal. There was a serenity in the way he seemed to flow up the underside of a boulder before reaching the top. After, there was a shot of him meditating on the summit. Neither the climb, nor the view, nor the danger had been the objective. For him, the mind-state had been the objective.

It had been beautiful and poetic, and watching him, I couldn't help but consider the similarities with karate. The danger of getting hurt can certainly help to focus the mind. I was wondering if danger is particularly helpful or necessary. After all, there are plenty of other ways to bring about a Zen-like state – tea making and flower arranging spring to mind – or sitting on a cushion and staring at a wall. But does some jeopardy help by making it all the more necessary to stay in the zone? I was still pondering this fascinating question when the presenter announced that shortly after filming, the climber had died in a flight-suit accident. I guess I had my answer.

In our discussion, we spoke of how science and tradition seem to be converging, but there's still some way to go. In this programme about neuroscience, there had been so much that corresponded with the Buddhist viewpoint that it would have made a great advertisement for Zen. Here's just one quote from the presenter, David Eagleman:

Given the brain's centrality to our lives, I used to wonder why our society so rarely talks about it, preferring instead to fill our airwaves with celebrity gossip and reality shows. But I now think this lack of attention to the brain can be taken not as a shortcoming, but as a clue: we're so trapped inside our reality that it is inordinately difficult to realize we're trapped inside anything.

As part of what he calls 'The illusion of reality' he showed how our minds create our own versions of the truth. How sensory information is adapted to fit our existing model of the universe. How we don't perceive objects as they are, but as *we* are. And what we think is happening out there is all actually happening in the brain:

Everything you experience – every sight, sound, smell – rather than being a direct experience, is an electrochemical rendition in a dark theatre [the brain].

As well as plenty on the nature of illusion and reality, he touched on impermanence and how everything, including ourselves, is 'empty' of fixed form:

The experience of your conscious awareness, right now, is unique to you. And because the physical stuff is constantly changing, we are too. We're not fixed. From cradle to grave, we are works in progress.

I asked Mike whether he felt it was useful to try and explain the benefits of zazen in Western terms. Mike mentioned Nishijima Roshi's belief that sitting in zazen balances the autonomic nervous system, which is beneficial for body and mind. However both traditional and modern explanations are all what David Eagleman calls 'models' on which to base things. It was a good reminder not to get too hung up on explanations, especially not at the expense of experience.

The third sitting was a short one, a single half-hour session. But it was hard. It seemed my hips had grown used to sitting for an hour and balked at the idea of going on any longer. For the last ten minutes, I sat with my jaw clenched waiting for the bell.

The one-hour lunch break did my hips some good and I managed the first session well. However by the second, a serious discomfort settled in my left hip and turned quickly to pain. From training we come to know the difference between training pain and injury pain. Training pain is something you can push through to make you stronger. Injury pain is something you must avoid, because forcing an area that's already damaged makes you weaker. Training pain can be intense – the final lap of a field, the extra rep on the bar, the last ten seconds of a fight. It can hurt a lot, but the pain is of your own making. Injury pain is different. It's a signal that all is not well. If you ignore it, or push through it, you'll simply make things worse and set yourself back for weeks in your training.

I was forced to move and tuck a second cushion under my knee for support. It saw me through to the end of the session, but I felt despondent and weak. I wondered how the last twenty-five minutes would feel. We had a short break and I took another cup of coffee.

Sitting again, the pain quickly returned and gripped my leg from the hip to the knee. I popped the support cushion under and it helped a little, taking it back from pain to discomfort. In the last fifteen minutes, I was aware of feeling a little sorry for myself. I was slouching on my cushion like a schoolboy waiting for the bell. I got annoyed with myself and tried to re-engage into what we were doing here. I wasn't sitting in front of a wall for three hours at the weekend for no reason. I was here to... to do what? To train my mind. To sharpen my focus. To develop my karate.

Suddenly, I was back in the dojo, on the front two knuckles of my fists, doing 'just one more push-up' as Sensei Gavin likes to say, over and over. And then I was back in the Shady Glade at summer camp, overlooking the field where the gradings take place, where I had seen so many students on the edge of exhaustion refocus their minds and convince themselves they did have something left, after all. I'd done this myself countless times, it has become the norm for me in my everyday training. Now I simply needed to access this mind-set on a cushion.

I recalled what Mike had said about zazen not being static but active. I thought of my state of mind when I know I'm good, when I'm sparring happily and there's a feeling like I'm balanced on a razor's edge, that I've got my opponent under a beam of stadium floodlights and whatever he does, I will catch him. There's a sense of poise, of being balanced on the cusp of movement, not static but active, knowing that I can strike at any moment. I accessed this mind-set, squeezed my core until my posture was tall and erect, and focused my mind like I was sparring. A surge of energy came and I went with it. This was, for me, after all, a martial exercise. I'd been a bit complacent in my sitting, too passive and soft. This was hard work, physically as well as mentally. This isolation of the mind was a good way to train the brain because there was nowhere for it to go. I focused my energy, my will, like a snake in the dark, waiting for the tiniest movement to disturb the air... and waited. My hips were barely registering now. I felt hyper alert and alive in the moment. This continued until the bell and after, I wondered if I'd turned a corner. Or had I simply clung to a mental game to see me through a difficult sit?

The next day I rested my aching hips. But the day after, I sat again and focused again on this sparring mind-set and took care to hold a new rigor in my posture. This wasn't sitting relaxed and balanced, this was balancing on a knife-edge. Three things crossed my mind while sitting. One, I felt like Musashi in his Book of Five Rings – watching his opponent, sword raised, ready to strike without a moment's hesitation. Two, for the first time, this felt like karate training instead of Zen training. I'd been feeling a little guilty about taking time away from karate, but this was enough to convince me that I was training. It wasn't that it was particularly physically harder, it just felt more active. And third, I shouldn't have been thinking, should I?

I attended one more day-retreat in May, just a few weeks before the big one in Scotland. It was a sunny day and I left the house feeling happy and carefree. But things began to unravel for me soon after. I went without my bag, thinking I didn't need it, but I'd forgotten my cushion. I had to make do with what I could forage in the community centre. The sitting was better this time and I managed the three hours with less fuss and mental turmoil. But when I got home, I couldn't find my wallet. After hunting for several hours, I rang the bank and cancelled my cards. I went online and ordered a new driver's licence and bought a new wallet.

Throughout the next day I felt uneasy, thinking someone had my wallet. My identity and credit cards were in someone else's hands, potentially a criminal's. It wasn't like me to lose my wallet. I couldn't remember ever losing a wallet before. The feeling of unease remained for the next few days and a heavy feeling in my chest, a mild depression. I was surprised that a wallet had affected me so much. I got a bit cross with myself and wondered why I was feeling so down? Eventually, I realised the loss of the wallet coincided with another, far greater loss that had happened exactly a year earlier.

Charmaigne and I had been in the process of adopting a child and we had come very, very close. A little girl had stayed with us for nine months until, just days before the final adoption hearing, a new member of the birth family had come forward. The unthinkable had happened, and after a bruising court battle she had been taken from us. It had been a period of incredible frustration, a feeling of powerlessness, a wrenching loss. Everyone said I'd handled it really well. I'd met the birth family and assisted in the hand-over. It had been the right thing to do. I knew I'd acted correctly, and yet there was something more and I wasn't sure what it was. We'd had a couple of sessions with a grief counsellor to help us through it, and it had been useful. I booked another meeting with her. She explained that certain times of the year can trigger memories of difficult times. The months the child had spent with us were happy memories, it was only losing her that had been heart-breaking. The counsellor said the first anniversary of a moment like this is often the worst but it can continue throughout life. It was good to know this and feel a bit more prepared.

My thoughts turned back to my life here and now and I wondered about the retreat coming up in Scotland – the big one, three days at a place called Anam Cara near Inverness. The others said it was a special place, set in a glorious landscape. I'd been to Inverness a couple of years earlier and spent New Year in a farm cottage surrounded by woolly Highland cows. It had been a magical trip and my first visit to the Highlands. I was excited to go again. Then I recalled that Tom had said the first sitting (before breakfast) was forty minutes straight. This sounded like a heck of a long time to me. He'd joked that you could hear stomachs rumbling in chorus, and I wondered if I'd be able to avoid thinking of food for forty minutes? I guessed we'd all find out soon enough.

ANAM CARA

On the way to Luton airport for my flight to Scotland, I wondered what the hell I was doing. Why on earth was I travelling all the way up to Inverness to stare at a wall for three days? There were so many better things I could be doing with my time. Still, it was too late now and as the taxi got stuck in traffic, I dug into my bag for something to read and take my mind off these negative thoughts.

I found a document that Charmaigne had asked me to look over. It was an introduction to a little girl that the adoption services wanted us to consider. I'd seen several other children recently and they had all been lovely, but none had felt quite right. Or perhaps I just hadn't felt ready to go again.

But this little girl was different. Her birth had been traumatic and the doctors had been worried about her for some time. But she'd pulled through. And now she had a foster carer who described her as a happy baby, who liked to be held and placed on her tummy so she could look up and see what was going on. I saw two bright eyes sparkling out of her photo. I felt a surge of admiration for this tiny child who, despite such a difficult start, had pulled herself through and now seemed so cheerful about life. I hoped to meet this little baby warrior when I got back to London.

Luton airport was crowded and chaotic, with building works going on outside and masses of people queuing for coffee and bacon rolls. I was pleased to see Matt from the Dogen Sangha. He was the most experienced student and a kind of unofficial sempai (senior student) – a hypnotherapist and counsellor who was very knowledgeable about all sorts of meditative practices. At first I'd thought Matt was a bit reserved but on getting to know him better, I realised this was just his manner. He had a wicked sense of humour and was great company. Better yet, he was happy to talk about Zen for hours and share his knowledge with me.

For a long time I'd considered sitting in Zen a largely mental endeavour, especially compared to karate. It was something like trying to isolate the mind-set of being 'in the zone'. Like training the mind to stay present in the moment. But Matt, like Mike, seemed to consider zazen far more physical than that, bringing things back to body and posture. He introduced me to the novel idea that it's not always the mind that leads the body. Things can easily be the other way around. For example, pain in the body can cause the mind to wander off to forget about the pain. This made a lot of sense. After all, how often are we short with people and snappy when we're in pain, or tired, or dehydrated, or ill? Mind and body are one and therefore act as one, inseparable. What we should do – and do do in zazen – is attend to the body and relax it, so the mind can quieten too. We wind back and slow down the cycle of mind and body spinning out of control.

Inverness airport was tiny and surprisingly crowded. We met two other travellers heading for the retreat and went to the taxi rank to share a cab. The taxi driver didn't know any place called Anam Cara, and telling him the address 'Upper Leachkin,' didn't seem to help. Fortunately a supervisor appeared who did know Anam Cara and he told the taxi driver the location. I noticed he didn't pronounce it 'Leach-kin' (as I had) but 'Larkin'. The taxi driver nodded, saying 'Ah, the place with the grass roof,' and moments later we were speeding along the main road to Inverness.

Soon we passed the little farm with the Highland cattle where I'd stayed two years earlier. Then the pulping factory with the chimney that blasted steam high into the air, day and night. My memories of the area were of glorious winter scenes – crisp blue skies, silver fields of frost and pale, glittering lochs. But now the gorse was out in splashes of vivid yellow across lush green fields.

Soon we were in Inverness, beautiful and austere, all shades of slate and charcoal grey astride the black river Ness. Then up the steep Leachkin Rise – which comes from the word for 'Loch', apparently. I was thinking how peaceful it was up here, far from the madness of London, when my phone rang. It was Charmaigne. She was in Sainsbury's and she wanted to know which cheese I wanted. I tried to answer in a whisper so my fellow Zenners wouldn't hear. I told her not to worry, I still had an unopened pack of Gruyere in the fridge.

The hill was 600m above sea level and Anam Cara was perched on top. The taxi dropped us off and the first building we came to had the grass roof that the driver had mentioned. This was the meditation hall, and the crowning glory of the place, with huge open sides of glass that offered stunning views down the hill. The rest of Anam Cara was a collection of timber-sided cabins on a croft, surrounded by woodland with mountains to the south and the Beauly Firth to the north.

Anam Cara is Gaelic for 'Soul Friend' – someone with whom you can share your innermost self, mind and heart. It's run by a friendly chap called Alistair and his wife and a small team of volunteers who come and go, living and working for a while before moving on. There's a cheerful, friendly, caring atmosphere without the slightest hint of ultra-spirituality that you might worry about.

The place holds a programme of events throughout the year for yoga, Zen and various holistic practices. I noticed feathers and markings that reminded me of Native American culture, and later learned that they ran regular courses in Shamanism, a practice dating back to the times of the Celts and Picts in ancient Britain.

The next building we came to was the office, a crooked little log cabin with a friendly young woman inside who booked us in and showed us to our accommodation. I was sleeping in a caravan, but you wouldn't know it because it had been clad in timber. My room was just big enough for a bed to fit end to end. It was colourful and cosy, but the walls were paper thin and I could hear the chap next door every time he cleared his throat (which was often).

Near me was the kitchen, which is always handy, and the lounge-diner where we would meet for food and talks. A chef had been brought in to cater for the event, a friendly woman called Sky who was all set to prepare vegetarian food for us. Other little buildings were tucked away in various nooks and crannies around the croft, including an 'Earthlodge' buried into the hillside, made with thick stone walls and used for shamanic rituals and ceremonies.

That evening I met more Zen practitioners from Bristol and Glasgow and, to my surprise, two from near my home town of Worcester, Dave and Sylvia. I hadn't known there was enlightenment in Worcester, assuming it to be a black hole in matters of the Buddha-dharma, but apparently these two sat together regularly and formed the Midlands chapter of the Dogen Sangha.

Dave was a friendly chap who I got on with right away. He was into racing motorbikes. Well, he was from the Midlands, after all. Sylvia was an elegant silver-haired lady who'd known Mike for years. She would be in charge of the daily routine during the retreat and she seemed to know exactly what to do. Fortunately for me, Sylvia was one of those people who takes everyone under their wing. As a newbie, I was happy to be there because I had no idea what to expect. I'd heard about the silent eating and the serving I'd have to do and I didn't want to mess up. I confessed to Sylvia that it was my first time and she promised to keep an eye on me.

That evening there was an informal meal and a short opening ceremony in the meditation hall. We were told to pick a position and a cushion and this would be ours for the duration of the retreat. I fancied a window seat so I could look out over the glorious Highlands. But what if the window seat threw me badly? I'd have to put up with it for the whole retreat. I decided to play it safe and stick with what I knew best… a wall.

I found a spot by the entrance that seemed like a nice out-of-the-way place to be, but I soon found out it was far from ideal. Mike also took up position by the entrance and sat looking out over the whole congregation. Not only was I right under his nose, but he'd be looking over my shoulder for the duration.

Mike said a few words to welcome us and set the tone for the next three days. He asked us not to think so much about getting something from the retreat, but rather to simply allow our minds and bodies to settle. Next came a brief opening ceremony: three prostrations to the Buddha statue in the centre of the hall. Each prostration involved kneeling down, placing the elbows on the floor and touching the forehead to the ground, then raising the hands, palms up.

The sitting itself was only half an hour. Sylvia had advised me to start slowly and avoid anything too challenging. I knew it was good advice. I put a cushion under my knee for support and sat in a simple cross-legged position – no half-lotus attempts on this retreat. Even so, my left leg and hip went to sleep quickly and by the time the bell sounded to finish, I couldn't feel my foot. When I rose, the entire left side of my body from the hip down was paralysed and I dragged myself out of the meditation hall by will alone.

Supper was vegetarian food. I was expecting lentils and brown rice but Sky had rustled up some Lynda McCartney sausages which tasted really good and some hearty pudding that went down a treat.

Mike announced the next day would start early and cautioned us against staying up late and chatting. I was very aware that I'd be sitting for far longer than ever before and I'd need to keep up my energy up throughout the next three days. Tomorrow's wake-up bell would sound at 6.20, so I needed no further convincing.

In my cabin, I managed to get warm and comfortable and read Dogen for an hour, until tiredness came and I turned in. I slept soundly until the tinkling of the morning bell, drank some water, did a little stretching and made my way to the meditation hall in time for the 7am start. This would be a forty-minute sit, far longer than any I'd done before, and on an empty stomach. I wondered how I'd manage.

To my surprise, the time went quickly and my legs felt fine. The night's rest and the empty stomach made it an easy sit, with less going on inside the body. It was equally pleasant on the next two days. I decided to try sitting at this hour at home, before the body gets busy digesting food and the mind gets caught up in the day's events, and it has become my preferred time to sit.

Breakfast was the first of the silent meals known as Oryoki. The name refers to the nested lacquer bowls traditionally used in Zen monasteries, with a strict etiquette for serving, eating, washing and rinsing. We stood behind our chairs and waited for Mike to sit. He clicked two wooden blocks together and we chanted the first four lines from a printed sheet. The words were in Japanese but I recognised some Indian names in there. These were four places associated with the Buddha's life: Kapira (Kapilavastu) where he was born, Makada (Magadha) where he was enlightened, Harana (Varanasi) where he taught, and Kuchira (Kushinagara) where he entered Nirvana.

Our appointed servers dealt out the cereal and porridge and

we chanted a bit more. Even for a beginner, it was easy to get in time and the deep, hypnotic monotone verses reverberated in a very pleasing way. A couple of the ladies went up a notch in pitch and created a hint of harmony, but the great thing about a chant is how easy it is to get in tune with everyone else.

Next we raised our bowls and chanted a bit more before tucking into our breakfast. We ate in silence, speaking only to ask for the butter or request another dollop of porridge. I found it strange and unnerving, like an awkward silence that needed to be filled. Ironically, I'm not normally the most sociable of people, but I liked my fellow Zenners and I wanted to chat with them. Fortunately the others, who'd done this many times, seemed content to eat in silence. Later they assured me that I'd get used to it. The silent eating prevented feeling the need to make conversation and preserved the stillness and introspection of the meditation, which I could appreciate.

Life in London, and in most places now, is pretty hectic. This was a rare chance to spend time away from it all, with like-minded people, in a community that comes together to help the individual to achieve this stillness, at least for a while. I could certainly see the merit in that. I ate carefully, making sure I wasn't still tucking into a stack of toast when everyone else had finished. There was a short closing chant called 'In Praise of Returning Water' which celebrates the rinsing of the oryoki bowls, traditionally done at the table by each diner with the help of a server and a bucket. In practice, our bowls were whisked away to the kitchen for a traditional British wash-up and dry with a dish cloth. All things considered, I felt we'd retained the spirit of mindful eating rather nicely while accepting the reality of our situation. We were, after all, on a farm in Scotland rather than in a Japanese monastery.

After breakfast came 'Samu' – a work period involving light chores around the farm like weeding, or moving gravel from one place to another in a wheelbarrow. It felt good to be doing something physical after such long periods of stillness.

In the first talk and discussion, Mike covered a passage from Dogen about mountains walking. *The Blue Mountain is always walking. The East Mountain tip-toes across the water*. This kind of poetic imagery is typical Dogen. It sounds surreal, beautiful, crazy, and yet somehow you have the feeling there's a deep truth in what he's saying.

What is he saying? Mountains are a symbol of permanence. In fact, it's hard to think of anything more solid and immovable than a mountain. But Dogen has already assured us that in reality nothing is permanent. Everything in the whole universe is always changing – mountains included. He uses preposterous imagery to shake us from our conditioned thinking about permanence. He might as well say mountains do handstands and cartwheels. But is he right? Do mountains move?

If we watch them for long enough, sure they do. Just as continents shift and stars grow and die. Even watching a mountain for a few hours or a few days, we can see changes in it: vegetation, landslides, animals coming and going.

Shortly after this talk, I watched a show on National Geographic that said the Rockies were relative newcomers to North America. They were, in fact, the third set of Rockies to have appeared on the continent.

More importantly, when we walk in mountains, what we literally see through our eyes is the mountains moving past us. From our point of view, the mountain are moving. From the mountain's viewpoint, we are moving. Dogen's point is, in the relationship between ourselves and the outside world, it's not just us or 'it' that's changing. Both sides are changing. Everything is always changing.

I felt moved and uplifted by Mike's ability to bring clarity to Dogen's poetic words. I felt inspired and encouraged to keep listening and learning. The passage was really about being open to new viewpoints. About not holding onto big, fixed ideas, immovable as mountains. These can be huge barriers to progress and understanding. In the West, moving mountains is also used symbolically to denote huge effort. But I liked this usage as well and I felt it was connected. To make big changes, we must first see that they are possible.

In karate, beginners often arrive with surprisingly fixed views. You'd think someone with little or no experience would be the most open to learning, but it's often not the case. I've seen teachers and senior students with years of experience offer advice that beginners refuse to take. Often they think they know better. Or sometimes they just seem unable to do what's suggested. Perhaps they take it as criticism, and they're unable to move beyond this. If they continue into the higher grades, they start to become more flexible in their thinking and more able to take advice. Less obstructed by their own ego. But some never overcome this and they tend to leave before reaching the higher levels.

Once a fighter's view opens up to all possibilities, the sky's the limit. I've seen students achieve things that would have been unimaginable just a few years earlier. Students who struggled at basic gradings and yet nailed the hugely demanding black belt test and the brutal 30 Man Kumite. Mountains didn't just move, they got up and walked and skipped over water.

Lunch was another half hour of what felt to me like awkward silence, and not a very relaxing way to eat. I wondered how long it would take to get used to it. Still, I consoled myself with the fact that I was learning a new ritual. And in the future, if I ever found myself in a strict Zen temple, I wouldn't embarrass myself.

Mike's second talk was more of a discussion, and the tricky subject of enlightenment came up. Some compared it to the Christian term 'revelation' – a form of sudden and deep spiritual awakening that brings about nirvana, a kind of blissful inner peace and happiness. Several people had read of such experiences in books by respected authors. Mike was clearly sceptical. They insisted that this sort of Satori (sudden awakening) was possible. Mike remained polite and non-committal. They argued on, and I began to feel uncomfortable. Not because I don't like arguments – a good argument can be very enlightening – but because the Japanese way of teaching had seeped into me from the martial arts. Open disagreement with a sensei is just not something you do. If you doubt or disagree, you keep it to yourself. Park it, and do as you're told. As a Westerner, you may think it's unhealthy to suppress your own ideas. But it can be equally unhealthy to pour out your own ideas at the expense of being exposed to other views. After all, if you're trying to learn or understand a skill or practice that someone has spent twenty... thirty... forty years perfecting, then why not shut up and listen? Your own ideas are more likely to get in the way than anything else.

Asked to justify his opinion, Mike's patience came to an end and he let them have it in no uncertain terms. He spoke vehemently about the current fad for mindfulness and how it was promising people spiritual experiences in two weeks, a yoga instructor's certificate in six weeks, all of which undermined the true nature of practice, where progress is slow, and mastery takes a lifetime.

This resonated with my views on martial arts, where students go on the 'seminar circuit' and train with twenty world-class masters for an hour here and there. This is not study, this is just collecting trophies. Mike warned against a pick-and-mix mentality where we only accept what we already believe. We carry a model of what we believe something to be in our heads. When we learn something new, we put it beside this model. If it fits, we accept it. If it doesn't, we reject it and go on searching. I knew from experience in karate that to penetrate a subject deeply, you must find a master you trust and do as they say, whether you like it or not. Give up what you think is the truth, just for a while, and see what else you can discover. After all, if you never empty your cup, how can you ever fill it with anything new?

My biggest leaps all came from doing things I really didn't want to do. Facing fears. Seeing how debilitating fear can be. Learning how the things I feared most hurt far less than the fear itself. Paying attention to details, the smallest, seemingly most irrelevant details, and discovering this made the biggest difference of all.

Some of the other participants still disagreed with Mike and insisted there was a place for this sudden enlightenment. Mike pulled no punches in setting them straight and I was glad he wasn't speaking to me like that. It was unnerving and unsettling but I was glad to hear exactly how he felt. Mike left us in no doubt how pointless it is to dream of unattainable goals, including a life of permanent inner peace and nirvana. In a day and age when everyone gets a say, no matter how 'expert' they are, or aren't, it was good to hear a master being unequivocal about the way forward. Afterwards, Sylvia approached me and asked how I felt about the rather heated discussion. I guessed she was worried it might have put off the delicate newcomer. I assured her, quite the opposite – I'd found the whole thing electrifying.

I've trained with enough karate masters to know that greatness can be many things. It can be uplifting and inspiring, and it can be unpalatable and scary. Great teachers can be tough, demanding and ruthless, as well as brilliant, generous and caring. They have their own personalities, and they keep them. There are plenty of teachers out there, but few masters. If you want to learn from a master, take what you can get and take the rough with the smooth. The experience of deep personal change is rarely nice and pleasant, so do yourself a favour and don't expect it to be.

As the talks and discussions went on, Mike stuck with the theme of avoiding fixed views. When Dogen returned from China and people asked what he'd achieved, he answered, 'Nothing'. Later, when pressed, he said, 'a flexible mind.' One of Mike's major written works is a translation of the Indian master Nagarjuna's work 'Between Heaven and Earth.' Even by Mike's own admission, it's heavy going. Nagarjuna writes in a long-winded and rather pedantic way, reminiscent of an old Greek philosopher, taking one view at a time and dissecting it this way and that before dismissing it as false. By the end of the book, Nagarjuna has left us with no 'true' view whatsoever. His conclusion is that we can only experience reality by the 'relinquishing of all views.'

We spoke for a while about whether such a thing is possible. As people, aren't we largely made up of our views and opinions? Surely it can't be right to give up or abandon a deeply held belief or principle? Isn't this what forms our personality? I wasn't sure what to make of this. Can we consider ourselves open-minded if our minds are closed and fixed on certain issues? I prided myself on being open-minded, but I also wanted to be a man of principle. Were the two mutually exclusive? I didn't know the answer but as usual, I had the strong feeling that Mike, and Nagarjuna, were saying something important. Something I needed to investigate more deeply.

In the next talk, Mike was conciliatory in tone. He explained that the reason he was so vehement before was because he felt strongly that too many people are promising too many miracles, especially these days when mindfulness is all the rage.

I knew that trying to achieve an enlightenment experience is not realistic. Dogen warns us against this frequently and in no uncertain terms. The beauty of Zen is not that it shows us something beautiful but allows us to see the world exactly as it is, unfiltered, raw, essential. This clarity of vision may be beautiful. Or it may not. It enables us to act naturally in each moment because we have all the facts as clear as they're ever going to be, unobscured by 'views' of our own making.

Mike pointed out, quite rightly, that he was here to teach Dogen's message. While we were here, we should suspend our other ideas and investigate Dogen's teachings fully. This was the whole idea of a retreat – achieving the peace and quiet needed to go deeply into things without distractions, and I couldn't help thinking he was right. Study one thing properly before moving on. You don't have to be a master, but you do need a good handle on something before you make up your mind about it.

In my last two sittings on the final day, I tried to pay attention to my posture. I sought out areas of stiffness and imbalance in my neck, back, shoulders and hips and made micro adjustments. Soon I felt wonderfully relaxed and free of the stiffness and niggles that often plagued me.

In another talk, Mike said, rather brusquely, that there was 'nothing spiritual about zazen'. It was a big statement and worthy of investigation. Unlike many other Buddhists and Buddhist schools, Dogen did not believe in reincarnation or rebirth. His view on living and dying followed a different kind of thinking, one that starts by saying there is no reality other than the present moment. We think of our lives as a continuous thread or stream, but in reality there is only what is happening right now. Life is life, right now. In our minds, life turns into death. But in the pure reality of the present, there is only life. Or only death. There is only the situation as it is right now.

I was quite happy to lose the term 'spiritual', despite the frequent use of the term 'spirit' in karate. To me, there's an important difference between the words 'spirit' and 'spiritual'. Spirit is clear and tangible, something akin to mood or emotions, like 'being in good spirits' or having 'fighting-spirit'. It's contained within the mind-body and simply part of the unconscious brain. 'Spiritual', on the other hand, is a word that promises a kind of dreamy, out-of-body experience beyond the realm of real life. And anything that sounds too good to be true, probably is.

It seemed zazen was closer to karate than I'd first thought. Body was more involved than I'd given it credit for. It's not just about isolating the mindset or the state-of-mind when engaged in karate, it is body and mind, a unison of action. The practice of zazen balances mind and body, bringing them into equilibrium and thus enabling them to act naturally together in each moment. The same could equally be said of karate, of kata, and indeed kumite. Rather than leading to somewhere special, they were a chance to experience something valuable in the act itself. A kind of unity that we rarely experience in other circumstances.

After the closing ceremony, we said our good-byes and people began to leave Anam Cara. I felt a sense of great calm and well-being. The retreat had been informative, exciting and fulfilling. My worries of sitting in torment hadn't materialised and I was surprised how good I felt. The timetable had been expertly structured, created, I imagined, by Mike after plenty of experience of his own. The sitting had been challenging, and difficult in places, but the breaks had been just long enough to allow my body to recover and go another round. The samu (work) had been invaluable in getting the muscles working and the blood flowing again. By rotating my sitting between left-over-right leg and vice versa, and including some kneeling, I'd managed to get through three long days unscathed.

With a few hours to kill before going to the airport, I retired to my tiny room to write up some notes. Before starting, I reread my earlier notes and saw what I'd written about our experience with the failed adoption. And all of a sudden I was thankful that the other guys had left the caravan and its paper-thin walls because I was in tears. I guess I'd gone into myself quite deeply and allowed these feeling to bubble up. During the retreat, some of my fellow Zenners had spoken of 'processing feelings' during zazen. I'd wondered what they were talking about. Most of my feelings had been happy thoughts about my favourite subjects: karate, strategy, tactics, weapons drills for summer camp, and occasionally, reminding myself that I shouldn't be indulging in thoughts but rather just sitting. And then this.

Where had it come from? I wasn't sad any more. I was angry – about the failed adoption. Angry with myself for 'coping so well', for 'doing the right thing', for being 'Mr Sensible' and not kicking off and going berserk. How could I have been so cold? Why hadn't I ranted and raved? What kind of father had I been? I would have done anything to protect that child, but in the end, I'd handed her over. I felt ashamed, knowing, even as I had these feelings, that if it were to happen all over again, I wouldn't do anything differently. They were just feelings, and I was just experiencing them.

On the flight home, I thought about my first experience of a Zen retreat. At the start, I'd convinced myself that I was wasting my time and I'd wondered what the hell I was doing there. This is fairly common at the beginning of any activity that's even mildly different from the norm. An in-depth event like this one takes us out of our comfort zone, and we don't like it. But by the end, I'd have happily gone on for another three days. I'd made several big steps forward in my understanding of zazen – the now 'active' posture, the deeper integration of body and mind, with the body playing a far greater role. And the idea that things are a lot clearer without 'spirituality' getting in the way. I had plenty to think about in the future, as I made my way back to my home and family, and that unopened pack of Gruyere in the fridge.

STEP UP, STAND DOWN

After the rigours of Anam Cara, I found I could settle into meditation at home more quickly. My muscles relaxed into place a little easier and I achieved a balanced upright posture a little sooner. My stomach felt relaxed and my breathing quietened to a whisper. I felt very still. I'd downloaded a handy app that timed my sittings for me and enjoyed the sound of the little bell resonating with its surroundings. Dogen's description of zazen came back to me: 'the dharma gate of repose and bliss'. I imagined I was returning to a special place, a secret glade or hidden cove that was all my own. Then I warned myself against indulging in too many fantasies. I should just enjoy my sitting and stop there.

In between times on the cushion, my thoughts turned to the next retreat on my calendar, quite different in nature, our annual karate summer camp. Yet in some ways it was similar. It would take place in beautiful surroundings, a little campsite on wooded hills outside Portishead, far from the hustle and bustle of everyday life. The only link with civilisation would be the noise of the M5, hidden behind the trees. The roar of the night traffic used to keep me awake, but over the years I've come to love this spot and now the sound lulls me to sleep like waves on the beach.

Summer camp is always a special experience. In some ways very relaxing, with warm sunshine (usually) and old friends. Great camaraderie, fun and laughter. But also hard work, long days of training, and for those grading, nerves that are always close by.

None more so than for Ed and Laila, who'd been preparing for this occasion all year. They'd both got themselves into great shape. Yet things had changed in sudden and dramatic fashion. Just a week before camp, in Laila's last sparring session, there had been an accidental clash and she had sustained a nasty injury to the face. With her nose bloodied, she'd carried on, but later an X-ray had revealed she had a fracture of the cheekbone that needed surgery. Laila's 30 Man Kumite had to be put on hold until she was fit to fight again. It was a major blow in more ways than one. For a lovely young woman to require facial surgery is horrible enough. But Laila seemed more concerned that she wanted to grade with Ed, to stand beside him and go through the test with him. We'd planned our training schedule to reach a peak at summer camp and it would be difficult to do it all over again. These were the new demons that Laila had to face.

Meanwhile, Ed had his own to consider as 30 male fighters lined up on the little green field known as The Field of Truth. He'd been shaken by Laila's sudden withdrawal. Strong bonds develop between people who face hardship together, and they'd enjoyed the idea of going through the test together. That wouldn't be happening now, and it was just one more thing he'd have to deal with.

There had been rain earlier and the grass was wet and soggy. We knew from experience that it would soon turn to mud and the fighting would be slower than usual. This could be a blessing for Ed because it affects the performance of the fresh guys more than the tired guy. Ed's line included just a handful of coloured belts before the start of the black belt section. From about half-way along, the black belts changed to include 'black-gis' – these were the fighters wearing the all-black suits that signified they had completed the 30 Man Kumite some time before.

Laila stood beside Ed at the edge of the field, waiting for the line to be counted and finalised. She'd had her facial surgery just a few days earlier and her nose was still in bandage. She seemed unconcerned by this, just intent on keeping Ed company right up to the last moment. Beside the two of them stood a fighter from Bristol, Dan Solomon, who would be taking his test at the same time. Dan was a big strong guy, in his late twenties, the perfect age to keep going through 30 gruelling fights. Ed, in contrast, was light and skinny and had just turned fifty. I wished Dan the best, but I worried for Ed. We all did. Laila, me, Gavin… the only person who didn't seem too concerned was Ed, who looked calm and prepared as he took his bow. This was good, his mindset was focused… at least for now.

Of everything in the 30 Man Kumite, this ability to stay present, to remain focused, to 'stay in the game,' is the most important of all. The fights get tougher and tougher as you get more and more tired, more hurt, and less able to fight back hard. This becomes a true test of self-discipline because the moment your mind starts opting out, you're in real trouble. Ed had remained present throughout his training, but this would be something else, a level of pressure that no fighter can ever experience beforehand.

There was a toss of a coin and Dan would start. Dan was usually a very busy and full-on fighter, which is hardly ideal for 30 consecutive fights. So I was reassured to see a very different fighter on the field today. Not only had he pared down his movement, he was playing the angles, picking his shots, and there was something more besides. He had a little swagger going on. Little touches of showy footwork. Not enough to tire himself out, just enough to put on a bit of a show and enjoy himself. This is quite simply the best thing that can happen to you because when you're enjoying something, you don't want it to end. Whether his enjoyment could last the full thirty minutes remained to be seen. Dan went through his first ten fights in this style and then it was Ed's time to begin. I'd half expected Ed to start a little stiffly – it's common because of the nerves – but Ed was moving and striking quite happily from the first moment. He continued this way for the next two fights but after the third fight was over, I noticed a slight drop in his shoulders. I wondered what this meant, but on resuming the fighting, Ed was still moving well, keeping his strikes crisp and clean, with his posture up and his chin safely out of the way. I shouted encouragement, telling him to continue just like this. Ed obliged and continued well until he'd completed his first ten fights. Meanwhile Dan had worked his way through the middle section of his line and reached twenty fights in good shape.

During the brief water break, I spoke with Ed. He was okay. He seemed tired but composed. I was happy with everything and told him so. Laila was beside him, and I could see her willing her energy into his tired arms and legs and stirring him on for another ten fights.

The fighting began again. By now any freshness was long gone and Dan and Ed were fighting on will alone. No amount of fitness can help you beat thirty fresh opponents, not of this quality. All it can do is allow you to continue and give you some chance to fight back. Ed remained composed and I was happy with his performance. Dan was into his last ten fights. The ground had been churned up and his once-white gi was brown and soaked through, but Dan's spirits were high. He roared himself on into his last five fights, which he completed in strong form. It was a performance to be proud of and the joy and relief were clear on his face.

But Ed still had ten fights to go. Again, I went to speak with him in the few snatched seconds of his final water break. He still seemed calm and focused. I told him the same as before, I was happy with the way he was fighting. He was staying in the game. Keep it up for ten more fights and it was done.

While Dan got his breath back at the side-lines, Ed went out to face his last ten battles alone. This was a formidable array of second and third dan black belts, and not one was going to let him by without a fight. Ed began well. He kept up his movement, posture and guard. Even so, he was getting hammered and I wondered how much more punishment he could take. Ed had been using low-kicks quite nicely but now he decided to throw a front kick. It wasn't something he'd used much in the past, however in our training he'd made good progress and it had begun to work. But now, tired and slow, against the smartest fighters, his front kick was getting caught and Ed was getting swept and taken down.

He rolled up from the ground readily enough and got on with it. But each time he threw the front kick, he got taken down. I yelled at him to forget the front kick and keep his kicks low. But Ed was like a kid with a new toy and he wanted to play with it. I wondered if he hadn't heard and yelled at him again to stop it. But Ed threw it again and got taken down, again.

Eventually, Ed stopped with the front kick and got on with the business of getting this thing done. And finally, at 'Fight 30', the redoubtable Tunde Oladimeji strode out and, in the words of one spectator, hit Ed with a thigh kick that would have felled an ox. Ed stumbled but remained standing. Better still, he fought on regardless, still present, and still reasonably tidy, all the way to the hard and bitter end. Then it was over and done. Ed bowed to Tunde, to the line-up, and to his chief instructors and returned on stiff legs to the shade of the overhanging tree, where Laila was waiting with water, ice-packs, and a huge grin.

In one sense, Ed's 30 Man Kumite had not been spectacular. He hadn't thrown spinning back kicks or pulled off any stunning moves. It had been a solid and creditable performance from beginning to end. But in another sense it was, for me, outstanding, because of Ed's mindset. Not just on the day, but on every day before that. His whole attitude. His whole approach. From his quiet entry into the dojo, to his black belt grading, to his constant commitment in preparing for the test. Through months of seemingly little progress to a feat that few fifty-year-olds could ever dream of accomplishing. This was an inspiring example of 'The Way' – and if anyone wanted to know how to achieve great things in karate, Ed had just made it crystal clear.

One of the most common observations among those who have finished the test is how different it is from training. There's simply no way to replicate the ferocity of the fighting – not safely, anyway. I asked Ed when he'd realised how things were going to be and he said it had been after the third fight. I recalled seeing his shoulders drop at that moment. His realisation of what was in store had come early, and yet nothing had changed. He'd continued as before and simply got on with the task. His success had been the result of a mindset that had stayed in the moment, not just for thirty minutes of hellishly hard fights, but every step of the way. Through good times and bad, thick and thin, hell or high water. And now he was free to reap the rewards.

What rewards, you may ask? Ed had passed a fearsome test

and now he could relax, at least for a while. The improvement in skill, fitness and confidence that comes with this feels like stepping through the doorway from a small room to a bigger room. In the big room there is more space to roam and explore.

One of the things I always notice, sparring with those who have completed the test, is how much more they enjoy their karate. Even though they can hit harder, they fight softer, more relaxed and playful. The lack of concern about getting hurt allows them to try new things and develop new skills faster than ever before. In many ways, it is the gateway to the highest levels of karate and the beginning of a new way of training that can last a lifetime.

Watching back a video of his fights, Ed was a bit disappointed that he'd been taken down so many times. I asked if he hadn't heard me yelling to forget his stupid front kick? He said he had, but he'd chosen to ignore my advice because he'd wanted to use his front kick. In the end he'd done his own thing, which I couldn't help admiring. Your coach and your sensei can only do so much for you. Out on the field, you're really on your own and you make your own decisions. If you want to throw your front kick, then go ahead and throw it. You're free to act as you please moment by moment, but you're also bound by the consequences of your action – just so you know.

Sensei Gavin said Ed had done every older fighter a huge disservice by showing them that being fifty is no excuse. Now we'd all have to keep working harder for longer – so thanks for that, Ed!

That night by the camp fire, Laila sat beside me and asked why I hadn't given Ed more coaching from the side-lines. It was a good question, and one I was glad she'd asked. I answered that apart from that damned front kick, Ed had done nothing wrong. He'd kept a clear head and read the attacks correctly. So I'd merely encouraged him and assured him he was doing fine. To instruct someone to use this punch or that combination is too distracting in the free-flow of a fight. By the time their mind can process your instruction, they will have missed their chance and been hit. Better to keep their minds empty of thoughts, so they can keep seeing clearly.

Ed wasn't in quite such cerebral mood. He'd brought a bottle of whisky to the campfire and quickly got stuck in. In recent years, a new tradition had emerged, throwing clothes onto the fire as a 'sacrifice' to summer camp. Sweaters, T-shirts, hoodies, even a bra had all gone up in flames. But Ed had decided to go one better and thrown his jeans on the fire. Standing there in his just his boxers, whisky bottle in hand, Ed was standing out again. And there was one more surprise. Normally fighters who've just completed the 30 Man Kumite had deep purple bruises up and down their legs. But Ed had barely a blemish, and not for the first time, I was struck by what a remarkable chap he is.

GENJO KOAN

After summer camp, my focus on karate eased off and I decided to go deeper into Dogen's unique brand of Zen. My first Goju Ryu master, Chris Rowen, used to say that you can explore a desert for hundreds of miles in every direction and you'll find nothing but sand. But if you drill down, you can learn all sorts of things about it. Beneath the sand you'll find rock, built up in layers, that shows how and when the desert was formed. Go deeper still and you might find fossils of sea creatures that reveal the whole area was once under water.

Chris was talking about studying one aspect of karate in depth. Going into detail in one kata, one principle, one movement. As the sword master Musashi says, 'from one thing, know ten thousand things'. A similar message is repeated by all the old karate masters of Okinawa. But these days so many clubs rush around gathering kata as if numbers were the aim.

I knew from personal experience how right Chris was. How getting one thing right reveals so much more. So I decided to do the same with Zen books. You might think Dogen's Shobogenzo would be the place to start. He was the founder of my school, after all. But his 'Treasury of the True Dharma Eye' was ninety-five chapters of densely packed musings, rules, poetic symbolism, Chinese references, word-play and a seemingly never-ending stream of contradictions. I knew I had to narrow things down – a lot.

There was one chapter, often featured at the beginning of the Shobogenzo, that crops up in all selected highlights of Dogen's writings. It was one I recalled from my own research as standing out for its brevity, depth and beauty. It's called 'Genjo Koan' and it seems to capture Dogen's views on the thorny subject of enlightenment most clearly. Today, I've come to view Genjo Koan as one of the most electrifying pieces of writing I've ever read. There are plenty of English translations, each one different, and at least two books dedicated to this short chapter. Some translators stick close to the original Japanese, which is beautiful and poetic, while others are more liberal with their interpretations and simplify extensively to convey the implied meaning.

The title Genjo Koan is a good example. The word 'Koan' comes from the ancient Chinese for a public document or case – something shared with everyone to express the truth. This is what Dogen is doing with this entire passage. Genjo Koan is translated variously as 'Actualising Reality', 'The Realised Universe,' 'Manifesting Actual Reality,' and similar. While the words vary, they are all pointing towards the same thing – some way of making reality real for ourselves. Reality not as we think it is, but as it actually is. I decided to study Genjo Koan like a kata, until I got a deeper grasp of it. And like a kata, the more I looked into it, the more it rewarded me. I read as many translations and commentaries as I could, and each pass of the text added a little more clarity. The piece was written early in Dogen's career as a letter to a lay person, a patron of the temple.

Perhaps this is why it's relatively succinct and clear – easier for a lay person to understand. Genjo Koan runs over only a few pages but it's packed with Dogen's power to get across an awful lot in a few words. Nishijima's translation opens as follows:

When all dharmas are seen as the Buddha-Dharma, then there is delusion and realization, there is practice, there is life and there is death, there are buddhas and ordinary beings.

When the myriad dharmas are each not of the self, there is no delusion and no realization, no buddhas and no ordinary beings, no life and no death.

The Buddha's truth is originally transcendent over abundance and scarcity, and so there is life and death, there is delusion and realization, there are beings and buddhas.

And though it is like this, it is only that flowers, while loved, fall; and weeds while hated, flourish.

When I first read Genjo Koan, I made the mistake of thinking the first four lines were the koan and the rest was Dogen's commentary. Fortunately, Mike put me straight on this and explained that the whole passage is a koan. Mike's version of the first four lines makes things a bit clearer:

When we look at the world subjectively, we can find concepts like deluded, enlightened, we can define what is Buddhist practice and what is not, we can give value to life and to death, and we can distinguish between buddhas and ordinary people.

But when we look at the world objectively, delusion and enlightenment cannot be found (i.e. are just abstract concepts), buddhas and ordinary people all have exactly the same physical makeup, and life and death are just states of matter.

The truth that the Buddha taught is not contained in the area where we analyse and discriminate, and so life is just living, and death is just dying, sometimes we are deluded and sometimes we are clear, some people are buddhas – awake to reality – and others are not.

And above all this, things are just as they are, sometimes as we want, sometimes not as we want.

Mike's version has stripped out some of the poetry but more than made up for it in clarity. And either way, what an incredible opening salvo! Dogen lays down the conventional view of Buddhism all nice and neat for us. Then tears it apart and leaves us with nothing. Then reassembles it with a new proviso. And rounds it off with a poetic flourish.

These four lines follow what Nishijima calls 'The Four Views' – a recurring theme in Dogen's writing. Dogen begins with a subjective viewpoint, which is how we usually see the world – from our own perspective. Second, he contrasts this with an objective viewpoint that's more scientific and analytical. This often negates the first view because when we investigate anything closely enough, we find nothing is ever completely fixed and permanent. Everything's always changing. Science and reason agree with Dogen on this, so how can we 'get' anything (even enlightenment) if there's nothing fixed to grasp?

Third, Dogen tell us the Buddhist Way is not to worry about either of these two conflicting viewpoints because neither is the whole truth. Believing 'nothing is real or fixed' is also false. It leads to a nihilistic tendency to think nothing matters, so why bother? Buddhism isn't like that at all. It's just about being more supple in our viewpoint. Taking each instance as it appears and judging at that moment, instead of falling back on preconceived ideas. The third view is judgement in reality, as it happens, in the moment. In action. The fourth and final view is often delivered in a poetic style that seeks to summarise the other three and resonate emotionally as well as rationally:

Flowers die even though we love them. Weeds spread even though we hate them.

This is Dogen's way of saying 'Accept the world as it is. It's okay to cherish flowers but don't cling to the hope that they will last forever. It's okay to dig up weeds but don't imagine they'll ever go away entirely.'

These four viewpoints can certainly be found in the martial arts. When we begin, we see karate as something we want to get for ourselves. We watch a movie or a demo and we think we'd like the power to break boards and kick ass. We want to know how to defend ourselves in the street. We want to feel strong and safe. This is our first view of karate. But when we get to the dojo and join a class, we discover it's nothing like the idea in our heads. There's a whole load of formalities which are a bit tedious. There's hard work, push-ups and sit-ups, and tons of basic exercises that all seem a bit pointless. And when you get hit, it hurts. None of this is what we imagined we'd be doing.

This is when a great many quit. Some realise martial arts are not for them. Others head off in search of something easier, and often go around in circles, searching for their original idea of karate like the 'hungry ghosts' from Buddhist scripture who are always ravenous and can never feel sated. They wander the seminar circuit, training for an hour or two in all the best martial arts, with all the best masters and building a CV that looks totally kick-ass – on paper. Every so often they rock up at a real dojo and get their asses handed to them. Because while they were listening to the wisdom of the masters, the dojo regulars were doing push-ups and hitting pads, and over the weeks and months this made them strong, fit and determined. Is it any wonder the hungry ghosts can't compete?

Slowly, the dojo regulars are beginning to look like the

fighters they had in mind when they joined. And beginning to see the reality of karate training. Yes, you can become a kick-ass fighter but it isn't as easy as it looks in the movies. You can achieve black belt, but it's going to take a lot more commitment than you thought. This is the third view. Reality in action.

In the fourth view, the line between karate and life has become blurred. Karate isn't something you think about but something you actually do. You take the rough with the smooth. You do the training you enjoy, and the training you don't enjoy. You know from hard experience that this is the only way. This is karate-do – the 'Way of Karate'.

Like Zen, karate doesn't give you anything special. You don't get to be a hero, kick ass and get the girl. You're more likely to get bruises and injuries of your own. So what's the purpose, and why bother? The only answer has to be that karate is its own reward. Stronger, fitter, more flexible, healthier. Mentally tougher and more determined. A deeper understanding of body and mind. These are not things that lead anywhere in particular. They are simply a better way to go through life as it unfolds.

Dogen goes on to warn us of the dangers of seeking enlightenment as if it were somewhere else:

Setting out to make ourselves one with reality is delusion. Reality making ourselves part of it is waking up.

It's pointless trying to get enlightened, because the trying gets in the way. But if we simply sit back and allow it, reality will make us part of itself. In the same way there comes a time in karate to set aside our own ideas of karate and simply do what is being asked of us – properly.

People who realize what it is to be deluded are called buddhas, and people who are deluded about what is real are called ordinary people.

This is fairly straightforward, as is the next bit:

Some people become clearer and clearer about reality. Some people become more and more deluded.

But this is interesting:

It is not necessary to be aware of being a buddha. We are still buddhas, and we go on experiencing the state of buddha, whether we know it or not.

It's common in Zen literature to hold up ordinary folk as examples worth following. Simple people doing simple things. Woodcutters and ox herders. Monks who have given up study for a life of 'chopping wood and carrying water.' This phrase 'chopping wood and carrying water' comes up a lot and it means taking care of the simple everyday things that make up life.
In short, you don't have to be a Zen monk to be awake to reality. We can all do it, all the time. We're just not aware of it. So maybe you're a buddha, and you didn't know it?

Dogen goes on to say that when we're seeing reality in the moment, without analytical thought or judgement, we're experiencing it directly, unfiltered and raw. It's not like taking a video and playing it back later, or drawing up a plan about how something might look in the future. When we're acting right here, right now, in the thick of it, we're seeing everything there is to see in its clear, natural form. Dogen puts it like this:

When we are experiencing things with our whole body-and-mind our experience is whole, it is not dual, like an image in a mirror, or the moon reflected in water, where we only see one side and can't see the other.

Then comes a very famous paragraph:

To study the Buddha Way is to study the self. To study the self is to forget the self. To forget the self is to be verified by all things. To be verified by all things is to let your body and mind fall away, and let the mind and body of everything else fall away. In this state all trace of realisation is forgotten and only this forgotten trace remains.

Wow. When we are wholly caught up in an action, we're not thinking about reality in our minds, we're fully engaged with it in our whole being. We are *doing* instead of thinking. In this state, there is no space for us to be aware that we are now 'awake' or 'enlightened' or in a 'Realised state'. So the only time you can be an awakened person (a buddha) is when you're not aware of it. How annoying is that?

When we first seek reality we are looking for it somewhere else. But when we are taught to experience reality by a true teacher it brings us back to our natural state.

The importance of a true teacher, a proper sensei, can't be overstated. We need someone to keep us grounded. Someone who has been this way before and made mistakes themselves. Mistakes they have learnt from, or learnt to overcome, probably with the help of their own sensei.

The famous Dogen analogies are coming thick and fast now. Next, he talks about the big question, the matter of life and death. And typically, he puts forward a viewpoint that is very different to the one we normally hold.

Firewood becomes ash. Ash cannot become firewood again. But this does not mean that we should only see a process in which firewood in the past becomes ash in the future. Remember that real firewood exists in the present. Past and future firewood are completely different from real firewood in the present.

This is a good example of how language and thought that appear contradictory in our minds is not so in reality. To be alive is the opposite of dead, right? Living is the opposite of dying. But is it? The Buddha saw that as soon as we are born we begin aging and moving – albeit very slowly – towards old age, sickness and death. That is what dying is: moving towards death. By this logic, living is dying.

Dogen tells us the Buddhist way is not to think of life as a process that stretches from the past through the present and into the future. Only the present is real. Everything else is just memory or projection. Concentrate on the here and now and you will see that in this moment, you are alive. That's the whole reality of your situation right now.

You might think Dogen's way of looking at things is so radically different from our own that to adopt his worldview would change your life drastically. But he reassures us it needn't be so:

When a person realises what reality is, nothing changes. It is like the reflection of the moon in water: the moon does not get wet and the water is not disturbed.

In Zen the moon is often used as a symbol of reality. The moon's light shines everywhere, illuminating darkness and ignorance. Seeing reality doesn't make us a different person, it just makes us clearer about life. Dogen goes on to say that everyone can see it, if they wish.

Even a small drop of water or a dewdrop on a blade of grass can reflect the whole of the moon's image.

Simply by looking at things with a mind unclouded by preconceived ideas, we can see reality just as it is. This may sound simple and easy, but the truth is it's almost impossible to see things without putting our own slant on them. Without screening them through our own lenses and filters. So Dogen warns us to beware of imagining, for one minute, that we are actually seeing the moon clearly:

When we feel confident that we understand reality, in fact we are far from it. When we are actually one with reality, we often feel that something is missing.

Dogen says an awakened person is more likely to feel like they're searching for the truth than have the smug satisfaction of thinking they know it all. This is undoubtedly true in karate, where even the most advanced masters continue seeking, never considering their art finished or complete, always adding fresh water to stop the pond stagnating. The same is true of all true artists. Cezanne painted the same mountain over 60 times. Monet painted the waterlilies in his garden 250 times. Picasso was never more productive than in his final years. An art is not a thing to hold or own. It's an itch that has to be scratched. A way that has to be walked each day. Next Dogen warns us of another important thing to keep in mind. Even if we see reality with an unclouded mind, we're still not seeing the whole of it. We can only see things from our own perspective, which is always limited.

If we sail out in a boat far from land, when we look around us, the ocean looks round. We cannot see that it has any other shape. But the ocean is neither round, nor square but has an inexhaustible array of characteristics, and to different species it must present a completely different image. But to our eyes it just looks round all around us.

Dogen says the ocean appears different to each thing that looks at it. To a fish it looks one way. Seen from above – from the view of 'the gods' – it looks different again. It has no fixed shape. Even if we were to map the entire ocean, from shore to shore, surface to floor, the water and the waves never remain the same shape. In the same way, the reality of the universe can't be captured in words, pictures or even thought.

The same is true of all things and phenomena in the universe. There are numerous ways of looking at situations from the ordinary person's viewpoint, and from the Buddhist viewpoint, but we only see and understand what is within our own experience. If we want to know what the natural and uninterrupted state of things is like, we should remember that they have endless qualities besides being a particular shape.

We can't hold the whole of reality in a thought. A thought is just a thought. Moreover, we are part of reality...

Our daily lives are an endless continuum of action, but we do not act in a void; our action always takes place in surroundings. The action cannot take place without the surroundings, because the surroundings always appear with the action. Action-and-surroundings are one indivisible whole.

This is important for martial artists. Our actions are always in relation to our surroundings – the floor, the air, the partner or opponent. A well-trained fighter is acting both as an individual and as one connected to his or her surroundings.

When fish move through water, however they move, there is no end to the water. When birds fly through the sky, however they fly, there is no end to the sky. Fish and birds have never, since antiquity, left the water or the sky.

We can't leave our real lives, although we often try! We can't escape our connection with the world around us.

We remain where we are, living in reality, even if our minds are elsewhere – which they so often are.

This being so, a bird or fish that aimed to move through the water or the sky only after getting to the bottom of water or utterly penetrating the sky, could never find its way or find its place in the water or in the sky.

If we want to understand everything and map-out life before we do anything, we'll never make a start. We'll never get a complete roadmap of life, so we must stop expecting one. We should simply set off from where we are now and go.

If we wait until we've compared every martial art against every other, we'll never get started on the real business of training. We'll never find the perfect dojo, just as we will never find the perfect partner or job or house. The best we can do is make an informed choice and get on with it.

The final part of Genjo Koan mentions one of the many koan stories that Dogen collected. It's a more typical koan, with a traditional exchange between master and student:

Zen master Hotetsu is fanning himself. A passing monk asks, 'The air is all around us and reaches everywhere, so why do you need to fan yourself?'

The master replies, 'You understand that air is everywhere, but you don't yet know what "reaching everywhere" really means.'

The monk says, 'What does it mean, then, to say that the air reaches everywhere?

The master carries on fanning himself.

The monk prostrates to the master.

Air is a metaphor for the Dharma – reality. The monk is asking why we need to make an effort to keep in touch with reality when it's all around us? The master doesn't bother explaining, he just keeps making an effort. Dogen is clear that the effort Buddhists make to keep in touch with reality is sitting in zazen. If they don't, they won't feel it, even though it's always there. Dogen goes on to say that the behaviour of Buddhists *turns the world into gold and the Long River into cream.* In other words, doing zazen makes the world a splendid place.

Dogen is advocating sustained effort, whether you're a student or a master. The parallels with karate are strong. We all know that as soon as we stop training, we start losing touch. Not just fitness, or technique, or things we used to know, but also the simple joy of training. Theory is all well and good, but practice brings the art to life. Even a little each day keeps us in touch. Every push-up, every stretch, every kick and punch, every kata and weapons drill, once learnt, must be maintained and cultivated, like a garden. It is both a splendid thing and, in truth, a bit of a burden – but one we should gladly shoulder. Like Zen master Hotetsu, we must keep fanning.

BEGINNER'S MIND

When I got back from the retreat in Scotland, I spoke with Charmaigne about the prospect of adoption. I discovered she felt the same way I did about the little girl we'd read about, and just as strongly.

Soon we found ourselves in front of the adoption panel for the second time. Our social workers had assured us it would be small and quite informal but by the time we entered the room, there were eight panel members and four social workers sitting around a large square arrangement of tables. The questions were friendly and delivered with warmth and smiles, but the circumstances were so important, potentially life changing, that it was hard to stay calm. Charmaigne and I answered as best we could and soon afterwards, we heard the good news. We'd been approved and the little girl would be joining our family.

Going to meet her for the first time was quite nerve-wracking. She was just a baby but she had the potential to change our lives. Would she turn out to be the little person I'd hope to meet? We drove to the flat where she lived with her foster carer and our social worker introduced us. The little girl accepted being held by Charmaigne but regarded me with caution. I played peek-a-boo behind Charmaigne's head and her round eyes tracked me. Then the ghost of a smile appeared on her lips. She was amused by the silly man's antics and I knew there and then that we'd get along fine.

Over the next week we spent more time with her, getting to know her routine and taking her for trips to the park and visits to our house until the day she spent the first night with us. Everything went well. She slept soundly with us, no hint of anxiety or disturbance. A little bundle of joy had returned to our house.

She was eight months old when she came to us and it was fascinating to watch her grow and change. Here was a person with no conditioning. She had her own personality, as all children do, but she had no language or social training of any kind. I was reminded of Shunryu Suzuki's book 'Zen Mind, Beginner's Mind,' in which he writes:

For Zen students the most important thing is not to be dualistic. Our 'original mind' includes everything within itself. It is always rich and sufficient within itself. You should not lose your self-sufficient state of mind. This does not mean a closed mind, but actually an empty mind and a ready mind. If your mind is empty, it is always ready for anything; it is open to everything. In the beginner's mind there are many possibilities; in the expert's there are few.

I was seeing this 'beginner's mind' at work and it was fascinating. Like any good baby, she knew all about the essentials. When she was hungry, she ate. When she was thirsty, she drank. When she was tired, she slept. If something upset her, she cried. When she wanted a cuddle, she put her arms up. Apart from that, she just lived day to day, moment to moment.

Babies have no shame. You can be enjoying a babbling conversation with one and all of a sudden, their faces go red and they squat and grunt, and you ask yourself: are they really doing what it looks like they're doing? The smell soon confirms it. But the baby is oblivious and happy to continue like nothing happened. It's nothing to be ashamed of and even the smell doesn't bother them. So why does it bother us?

You can argue that for the purposes of hygiene, we must learn to use a toilet and identify 'bad' smells and avoid them or clean them away. But a beginner's mind isn't the slightest bit concerned by this. And I can't help thinking how liberating it must be, not to have so many cares and concerns. Not to be embarrassed by this, or repulsed by that, simply because somewhere along the line we've been conditioned to think this way.

When you consider how many other habits and rules and pre-conceived ideas we accumulate over the years, is it any wonder that we're a mass of thoughts and feelings and worries and concerns and aims and things that aren't really fundamental to living life as we are, just at this moment?

Clearly we can't avoid the process of conditioning but we can be aware of it. And just how much of what we think is important isn't that important. And how much this conditioning affects our daily lives. We use conditioning in karate to achieve tremendous results. By repeating certain exercises we can condition the body to be strong and the mind to be determined. But if we are too conditioned, our responses become predictable and this can be a problem. The best fighters are adaptable and able to think on their feet. If something isn't working, they change it. Better still, they don't get stuck in a rut in the first place.

By the time our baby was learning to talk, she had a vocabulary of around twenty words that served her very nicely. 'Num num' was food. 'Ap-ul' was apple, and every other fruit – in fact anything that was soft, round and edible. One of her first words was 'up', with arms outstretched, indicating that she wanted to be picked up. 'Up' also came to mean going up the stairs, which she could do, one step at a time, very nicely. But when I held her hand to go downstairs she still said 'up' with every step, 'up... up... up...' – which was quite disconcerting.

Her unformed view of the world had begun to take shape, but the forms she used were still loose and a little undefined. She didn't believe in possessions. If she wanted my dinner, she fully expected me to share. Just as, if she had something to eat, she would offer me a bite. If she wanted a toy at playgroup, she took it. An older child might object and claim it was his, but as far as she was concerned, everything was 'ours'. And in many ways, she was right.

The whole world is ours. We are never apart from it. If I live in London, I can ignore problems in other parts of the world by telling myself they don't affect me. But if I see the big picture then everything affects me.

I think of myself as an individual. But I'm also part of a family and a karate club. When I think of the individual members who make up the club, I see a mass of individuals. When I think of the club as a club, every individual disappears. Where am I in this, now?

One of the classic Buddhist questions is 'Who are you?' If you look at a picture of yourself as a child, is it the same person you are now? Everything has changed. Your body has changed. Your mind has changed. There was, and is, something that is 'you' but that thing, whatever it is, or was, is not permanent. It has always been in a state of flux. Reality does have forms, but these forms are changing moment by moment. There is no permanence to any of it. So in some ways, how a child sees the world is closer to reality than how we see it.

Dogen and the Buddhist masters are not saying we should

go back to being a child. They are saying there's something important and fundamental in this unformed view of the world. The view before conditioning takes over. This 'pre-conditioned' state is natural and essential and free. Free of worries and concerns. Free from anxiety and depression. Free from unhealthy desires and unnecessary goals. Free from pointless fears and needless dreads.

Feed a baby, clean it and give it cuddles and it's perfectly happy. Take care of the essentials and stop getting caught up in everything else that doesn't matter all that much.

Buddhists aren't alone in singing the praises of babies. Taoists love them too. Lao Tzu said babies are in tune with the Tao. Despite being soft and helpless, they're not afraid of anything. Scorpions and snakes and all manner of wild beasts don't worry them in the slightest. Babies may be weak, but they have a surprisingly strong grip. And as every parent knows, they can scream all day without getting tired. This is true vitality! Babies don't need a reason to get excited. Little children can have fun from the simplest things, from simply being alive. Chuang Tzu said something similar:

The baby watches without being affected by what it sees, sits without caring where it is sitting, moves without worrying about where it's going.

It's unlikely Chuang Tzu was a parent because his description of a baby's body and heart are a little nasty – he says a baby's body is like *a rotting branch and its heart is like cold ashes.* (A rotting branch is weak and gives way easily, while cold ashes are 'cold' – completely unsentimental.) But Master Chuang concludes:

Being like this, neither bad fortune will affect it nor good fortune draw near. Having neither bad nor good fortune, it is not affected by the misfortune that comes to most others.

Something about a child's complete lack of concern is very appealing, don't you think? And it's not only ancient Buddhist and Taoist masters who are amazed by babies. My favourite neuroscientist David Eagleman explains that a newborn baby is literally more open-minded than an adult, with more potential to learn new things:

As many as two million new connections, or synapses, are formed every second in an infant's brain. By age two, a child has over one hundred trillion synapses, double the number an adult has.

As we mature, the number of synapses is pruned back by half. The ones that get used regularly remain while the ones that don't get used eventually weaken and are eliminated…

Just like paths in a forest, you lose the connections that you don't use. In a sense, the process of becoming who you are is defined by carving back the possibilities that were already present.

It seems a baby's mind is open and fluid, or 'plastic,' as scientists say – supple and open to everything. For example a baby, over time, learns to mimic the accent of its parents perfectly. A baby born in Scotland learns to speak with a perfect Scottish accent. It never sounds Welsh or Irish. Yet once that baby grows up and moves to London, it can't speak like a Cockney. And as every language student knows, you can spend years in another country and never achieve a perfect accent as an adult.

So we can see that it must be useful to retain some of the openness of a beginner's mind. To be, as Shunryu Suzuki says, like a dark sky that is never surprised or disturbed by passing clouds or sudden thunderbolts.

But how can we stay open and remain prepared? How can we recalibrate our minds to stop worrying and obsessing about all the wrong things? Suzuki's answer, like any Zen master's, is daily practice. Meditation… zazen... just sitting. As Dogen puts it: *Clear the mind of unnecessary concerns… shine the light inwards… let body and mind fall away and your original nature will manifest.*

WINTER CAMP

Laila's 30 Man Kumite test had been rescheduled for winter camp in October. Her training had been designed to peak in June and I wondered, could she peak again four months later? It wasn't as straightforward as you might think because there is a natural peak and trough in an athlete's performance over a year. Summer is traditionally a period of rest and recuperation, and not ideal for hard training. Plus, Laila had not one but two holidays booked before winter camp which would certainly impact her programme.

Then there was another question, more subtle, but perhaps even more pertinent. Had her injury rocked her confidence? She'd shown a little wobble during Psyche Week, and then she'd been through a traumatic injury. Would she be able to give the performance that I'd felt she was ready to give in June? We'd find out soon enough.

Laila devised a training programme for her holiday that included getting up early and running along the beach. It wasn't ideal but it kept her fitness ticking over. When we eventually returned to the football field for sprints and training with the big red kick-shield, she was in good shape. Good, but not great. Her footwork was a little shaky and she tripped a couple of times. Her striking wasn't quite as venomous as I knew it could be. We had just one more week to set things right.

I asked about her surgery and she assured me that she was completely healed. Was she able to take a stray knock to the face? The doctor had said her bone structure was no weaker than before. She looked as good as new, with no visible sign of the injury at all. She seemed confident, but beneath it I sensed a little something holding her back. I knew how good she could be. I'd felt her striking the pads all through the winter and I knew she had more to give. We went back to some of our more basic exercises to sharpen up her footwork. In our final week of training the footwork was much tidier and there were no more stumbles. The striking was solid and hard. There was nothing obvious, just a sense that she had more to give, somewhere. Could she access that extra something on the day?

Laila had won gold in kumite at our annual tournament for the last two years in a row. Expectations were high and now it was time to deliver, not for me, or Sensei Gavin, or anyone else, but for her own sake.

We walked across the training field and spoke about her mindset. She confessed to nerves welling up, surprisingly big nerves. I was glad she was being open about it and assured her that this was good. Nerves are important. Nerves drop adrenaline, and adrenaline enables us to perform at levels we can't normally reach. It's no coincidence that the world's top athletes set world records at the Olympics – it takes the greatest competition to bring out the best performance. Nerves are good, I reassured her – the bigger the better. Bring 'em on and ride 'em like waves. Catch a tsunami and it'll carry you all the way to the shore.

We'd spoken in the past about Jessica Ennis, the poster girl for the London Olympics in 2012. She was a great example of a favourite who'd had great expectations heaped upon her. It would have been all too easy for Jessica to cave in under the immense pressure, but she'd shone and taken gold. Laila had read her autobiography and taken some inspiration from it. Would she be able to shine too? We would find out soon enough.

One week later we were walking across a different field. It wasn't the traditional 'Field of Truth' at summer camp where the test normally takes place. There was no lush grass or overhanging trees to contain the action, just a stark windswept field with rough grass underfoot. We found a secluded corner and marked out an area that would become our temporary Field of Truth.

Laila listened to music on her headphones while she waited for her line-up to form. She appeared calm and determined. Gavin and Dan selected female fighters from green belt up to third dan and told five of the guys – all second and third dan level – to prepare with gumshields and mitts.

The first fight was against a smaller green-belt woman. Laila struck with a ferocious right hand that detonated on target. Her opponent winced in pain and Laila stepped back, allowing her time to recover. Another shot, and the same reaction. Knowing how hard Laila could hit, I knew the green belt wasn't being weak. These were seriously nasty strikes. A kick across the thigh had a similar effect.

The next few fighters got similar treatment and the pain was obvious on their faces. I was pleased to see that Laila wasn't piling in and punishing them, she was just issuing warnings and they were hearing her loud and clear. This made for a very measured pace for the first few fights. But then the brown and black belts came out and suddenly, Laila wasn't having everything her own way. Yet even against these tough fighters, she was never in any trouble. She seemed to be enjoying each encounter and remained more or less in control.

After ten fights she had a break and I went over to have a quick word. 'Everything alright?' I asked. 'It's tiring,' she complained. 'Is it? You're making it look easy,' I told her. 'Just keep doing what you're doing.'

Laila fought on and I watched, in awe of how well she was performing. What I saw was attention poised on a razor's edge and ready to strike at every moment. To lunge forward and throw a reverse punch is one of the most fundamental karate weapons, and it is so for a reason. Done correctly, this 'reverse punch' is devastatingly powerful. We all learn it. But Laila had made it her own. As well as forward explosion, hip-twist, accuracy and focus, she'd mastered the real key which is timing. Laila was catching her opponents on their way in, before their own punches had materialised. This means reading the opponent and having the confidence to fire the punch early – before the target is fully formed – in the knowledge that it will connect at the right moment. Again and again, I saw her catch people as they swarmed in and the power of her punch was such that it stopped them in their tracks. Laila also used the lunge to move back before any reprisals could come her way. This takes diamond-hard nerve, and it was so good to see Laila hadn't lost hers.

But no one gets to control the 30 Man Kumite. The test is designed to strip you of control, and then see what you have left. And now among the female second and third dans, Laila was facing the toughest women in the association. Too good to get caught, and too strong to be stopped, they fought in close and forced Laila to stand toe to toe and exchange punches, giving her a hard time of it. But even after twenty fights, she still looked in great shape. We spoke during her water break and again, she complained she was tired. I assured her she was fine. But we both knew what was in store in the last ten fights. Five high level male fighters were warming up. I told her to continue fighting the women just as she had been but when the guys came on, she would need to step up a gear. She nodded but I wasn't sure she'd heard me.

After a few more female fighters, the first of the men stepped out. As his first punches and kicks landed, Laila seemed momentarily rocked. He wasn't holding back and her own punches and kicks weren't having the same effect. Now she was on the back foot and for the first half of the fight she seemed hesitant. But then something clicked, some sort of acceptance, I imagined, and she got back into it. In the next four fights, each new guy seemed to go in harder than the last. Laila rode out the storm and fought on as hard as she could. The last of the male fighters, her old friend Simon Clinch, smashed two cracking straight punches into her and a lightning fast high kick – beautifully controlled – that brushed her cheek and told her to keep her guard up. After this thrilling fight, it was left to the two most senior women to finish the job. Through all this, Laila fought back strongly to the very end.

It was the performance I'd hoped for and, in truth, more. Laila had always been good but I saw her achieve a new level that day. Just like Ed's, her performance had been more than an impressive physical feat. I felt I'd witnessed an outstanding display of mindset and focus. I'd seen someone absolutely and completely engaged in every movement and every moment of every fight.

This wholehearted commitment had been manifest in 30 fierce fights, clearly visible for all to see. But I knew it had been equally present during the long hours of training, and the even longer days and weeks of being unable to train. It had been present in the times when she'd been forced to prepare in all the wrong circumstances – like being on holiday, away from the heavy bag and the Thai pads and the sparring partners that she needed, away from her sensei and her beloved coach! And I'm convinced the mental strength derived from such setbacks more than made up for the imperfect conditions. In fact, it gave her the spirit and will to deliver something very special that day.

ZEN AND KARATE

It's not supposed to happen, but sitting with the Dogen Sangha seemed to give me special powers. Quite unusual ones – like a better musical ear. I'd been playing the guitar on and off for thirty years, mainly for my own enjoyment, never getting much better or worse. I've never had perfect pitch but I can tune a guitar reasonably well using pitch pipes. The results are rarely perfect and if I use an electronic tuner I notice a difference – a kind of ringing clarity that I rarely get on my own. However, shortly after beginning zazen, and thinking how much I liked the resonance of the bell, I had the idea of tuning the guitar not by trying to match the note with my ear but rather by trying to match the resonant frequency of the string. I tried 'seeing' the wavelength in my mind and then matching it with the next string. The results were remarkably good and I got the ringing quality I normally only got with the electronic tuner. Was this a result of zazen, or simply an inspiration based on something it brought up in my mind? Who really cares? My guitar sounds better.

What else? I was relatively calm at home and a little more understanding, I think. A bit less shouty. Maybe. Another surprising thing it helped with was weight-training. By becoming more aware of the balance of my body, I noticed on my overhead press that the weight distribution between my feet was uneven. My right foot was pressing harder into the ground than my left. This meant my right side was doing more of the work while my left was underused. By putting a tad more pressure into my left foot, I went from my usual six reps all the way to ten – a new personal best. In my karate, I'd been working on rooting, which comes from making a solid connection with the floor. It's hard to explain and easier to feel, but rooting is an important facet of generating power at close range, when there's no room to move your whole body backwards or forwards. Think of a tree, rooted in the ground. The trunk is strong but the branches taper. By pulling back a branch and releasing it you can get a hard thwack from only a few inches of movement, but only because the branch is connected into the stronger trunk which is connected to the earth.

Rooting was a theme for me in my training. I'd thought I was pretty good, but when Sensei Gavin did a session on rooting I was surprised and disappointed by how easily he could shift me. Usually I know how to train to achieve improvement and don't need much telling. If I want to get fitter, I run. If I want to get stronger, I do weights. If I want to hit harder, I work the bag. This was different. Gavin is a big strong guy but even so, he was moving me so easily that I knew there was something more at work. I spoke with him at some length to get his take on it. He talked of alignment of force and visualisation of energy flowing both down into the floor and out through the hands. Interestingly, he said meditation would help me with this. I was dubious, but since I was doing it anyway I thought it couldn't hurt. After meditating one morning before training, I felt very centred and balanced during my kata practise. I was able to focus more clearly and deeply on one spot or line of motion before me, which helped to make my balance feel considerably firmer. I was also able to sink my weight better while feeling on balance.

Some weeks later we did a little more rooting practice. Pushing hands with Gavin I felt stronger compared to the last time, and he noticed the improvement. This encouraged me to keep on with my rooting training.

I began performing my kata in the style of tai chi, moving slowly and smoothly, taking care to ensure my feet were firmly planted in each stance and that my weight felt balanced with each movement. I pushed against walls, trees and posts from various angles, exploring the posture that delivered the strongest pressure. Trying to pay attention to the little things.

Then one day, as so often happens, the payoff for prolonged effort got delivered in one big heap. In training that morning, I felt full of energy. My feet seemed so fast and connected to the floor. Techniques seemed effortless, powerful and heavy at the same time. I practised a bo-staff kata and a nunchaku kata, and I felt very strong without trying. This can only come from subtle improvements in weight distribution, balance and connective tension.

In November we ran a kata tournament and at the end, Gavin, Dan and I also performed a kata. After judging kata all day, I knew it would look pretty lame if I couldn't perform well myself. So I practised the kata Seisan extensively. It's a tricky one because it has a difficult sequence, a knee-raise, kick, turn and stomp all performed while balancing on one leg. This takes a lot of doing if you want to achieve power and control. After a long day of judging, and a seminar and demo from two 3rd dan candidates, it was time to get up and do my thing. I suppose it's no great drama or surprise to say I gave a decent performance. Nothing went wrong. I felt strong and powerful, with good balance throughout. So did Sensei Dan and Gavin. But I noticed something in myself was definitely different. I felt calm and focused from beginning to end. I managed to inhabit the kata fully. It wasn't perfect. I noticed two tiny 'gaps' appear, both just nanoseconds in length. In one, after a sudden and dynamic turn, I felt a small lack of connection in the sole of my left foot. A wobble so small that no one would notice... except me. In the other, I noticed one particular chap in the audience, watching me. I don't know why. I shut him out instantly and the gap closed again. No performance is ever perfect. Perfection is the impossible standard we aim for but never achieve. However I felt my ability to stay present and focused in the moment was stronger than ever.

Some weeks later, after a hard karate class, we went through all the kata in the syllabus, one by one. With each new kata, any student who didn't know it dropped out and by the end, only the highest grades remained. This makes things difficult for the seniors because by the time all eyes are on a few of you, you're already tired from all the previous kata. Eventually, as the highest grade, I was on my own. Sensei Gavin asked me to perform a kata with the 6-foot bo staff. I hadn't practised it recently but this didn't seem to concern me. I picked up the bo and performed the kata. The result was rather good, even if I say so myself. Several senior grades commented afterwards and even Gavin managed to dredge up a compliment. But the interesting point for me was how easily I'd managed to simply focus on performing, and then perform.

Had sitting on a cushion and staring at a wall really made such a difference? It seemed it had. I tried to analyse my experiences of good focus. Thinking hadn't disappeared altogether – there had still been conscious thought, combined with unconscious thought and action. It had been more that unnecessary thoughts hadn't cropped up and gotten in the way. Those unhelpful thoughts that come from feeling self-conscious hadn't arisen. I hadn't stopped to wonder how well I was doing. My whole attention had been directed just to the task, and I believed I had 'just sitting' to thank for that.

KATA BY NUMBERS

My journey into Zen began to reveal more interesting connections between Buddhism and the martial arts. In the Goju Ryu school of karate some of the names of the kata are self-explanatory – 'Attack and Smash', 'Tear and Smash', 'Trapping Battle' – but others are simply numbers like 'Eighteen', 'Thirty-Six' and '108'.

These numbers are thought to refer to pressure points from TCM (Traditional Chinese Medicine) that can be used in combat to affect the body's flow of vital energy. Some of these points are fairly obvious. We know that striking the head or jaw can cause a neurological shutdown, temporarily stopping or at least changing electrical signals in the brain. Strangling an artery in the neck interrupts the flow of blood to the brain. Choking the windpipe prevents the flow of air into the body. A sharp rap on the solar plexus makes it difficult to breathe. However the Chinese system is complex, with pressure points all over the body, categorised along 'meridians' and linked to the functions of vital organs.

The classic martial arts text 'Bubishi' – known as the 'Bible of Karate' – lists 36 vital points that can be used to in combat, and over time this number was expanded to 108. Eighteen 'movements' is a recurring theme in Chinese arts and these movements were ways of striking at vital points. In reality there are hundreds of points all over the body and these can be used and struck in an almost infinite number of ways. So it can't be coincidence that the numbers settled on for the kata match significant Buddhist numbers from antiquity. They were chosen to strengthen the link between martial arts and Zen.

In Buddhism, like other religions and systems that teach young people, things are often broken down into numbers to make them easier to remember. When it comes to perceiving reality, we're told we have six sense organs: eyes, ears, nose, tongue, body (touch) and mind (which can generate its own perceptions). When these sense organs come into contact with things around them, they generate sight, sound, smell, taste, touch and thoughts. And even then, the early masters knew what our neuroscientists are telling us today – we don't perceive sight in the eye, or hearing in the ear, but rather we interpret these signals in the brain. This gives rise to six kinds of 'consciousness in the mind'. Added together, these three groups of six variables form what Buddhists called the 'Eighteen Elements' – Eighteen ways to perceive things. Eighteen chances to see reality as it is. Or eighteen chances to misinterpret reality and change it to what we'd rather it was. Either way, Eighteen is a significant Buddhist number.

So it's no coincidence that when the Taoists created a muscle strengthening exercise and attributed it to the breathing methods of an ancient Buddhist sage (Bodhidharma) they claimed he'd taught 'Eighteen' movements and made eighteen bone and marrow strengthening exercises.

You might think that for the Buddhist practitioner, Eighteen is a lot of ways to potentially be deluded, but it doesn't end there – not by a long way. There are two types of people who encounter these Eighteen Elements, Buddhists and lay-people. Buddhists have (at least in their vows) renounced desires, while lay-people remain attached to earthly pleasures. That means each of the Eighteen Elements can be either 'attached to pleasure' or 'detached from pleasure' – making Thirty-Six 'Passions'.

Each passion can be felt in the past, present, or future, so there are 'three time-frames' that add up to a grand total of one-hundred-and-eight.

So in Buddhism, people are said to have 108 Afflictions or Klesas, sometimes called 108 Defilements, Vices, Evils, Passions, or Earthly Desires (not really 'sins' because in Buddhism there is no requirement for shame). In short, there are 108 ways for delusion to occur.

You can imagine the old masters warning the young monks to remain alert. To stop assuming that what they think is real is actually real. To stop preconceived ideas and social conditioning obscuring what they really are experiencing. To stop letting thought get in the way of experience.

These significant numbers – Eighteen, Thirty-Six and One-Hundred-and-Eight – are all kata in the Goju system: Seipai (18), Sanseiru (36) and Suparinpei (108) –

(although the names are not classic Japanese but rather Okinawan derivations of Chinese numbers).

While Eighteen and Thirty-Six are not especially significant in Zen today, the number 108 is universally relevant in Buddhism. Wherever there are steps leading up to a temple, there are usually 108 to climb. Buddhist priests carry 108 prayer beads and at New Year, the temple bell is struck 108 times to see out the old and welcome in the new.

SWINDON SESSHIN

As the winter nights drew in, the sunshine of our last retreat at Anam Cara seemed far away and it would be many more months until the Dogen Sangha could do it all again. So there was some interest in holding a similar three-day retreat, a little closer to home. After a bit of research, a little farm near Swindon was chosen to host a winter retreat. A date was set in January and I booked my place. When the day came, I left work early on a miserable Thursday afternoon to get a lift in Matt's minibus, quickly christened the 'Zen Bus'. Darkness had fallen by the time we reached the place, nested in among modern housing estates just off the M4. This was far from the highlands of Scotland in more ways than one, but the farm was surrounded by trees and if you didn't venture too far, you could imagine you were in the countryside.

The owners were warm and welcoming. They seemed happy for us to do our own thing. They would be catering for us and did the necessary checks about who was vegetarian, vegan and gluten-free. The format and timetable of the retreat would be the same as in Scotland, which had worked well in the past.

Mike arrived soon after us and it was good to see him again. Some of the group had rooms in the farmhouse, near the meditation hall, but I'd been allocated one of the log cabins outside. It had coloured glass in the windows and looked very inviting. Inside it was freezing but there was a thick duvet and blankets and a heater that soon warmed the place and made it feel homely. Supper was informal, the food was good and tasty, with plenty of fresh bread baked on the farm. Then there was a brief opening ceremony with three prostrations to the Buddha to get things going. Mike reminded us to cast aside ideas of getting something and rather, to allow our minds and bodies to settle.

I found it hard to follow Mike's suggestion. I felt fidgety. Thirty minutes seemed to go on for hours. I wondered what the hell I was doing here. What was the purpose of it all? I could have been at home relaxing with my family but instead I'd chosen to come and sit on a cushion and stare at a wall. I decided to wait and let these feelings pass. They are common at the start of these events.

Afterwards, Mike repeated his advice to get an early night and be fresh for the morning. I knew how difficult it could be to sit properly when you're tired and I was about to follow his advice but one of our number, a young actor called Jaz, wanted to chat and we talked a little about karate and acting and didn't turn in until late. I got to sleep just fine, setting my phone alarm for 6.30 just in case I didn't hear the morning wake-up bell. But the farm's cockerel had other ideas and kicked off at precisely 4.05.

After three hours of fitful sleep, I woke to the tinkling of the bell and my groggy attempt to do a little stretching before the long sit. I was worried about my ankle. I'd strained it a few days earlier, while sitting. It sounds silly, I know, for a karate-ka to strain something on a cushion but quite frankly I was far more concerned about sitting than I was about karate. I'd learnt to cope with all sorts of exercises and painful blows, but in sitting there was nowhere to go and nothing to do. If you get an uncomfortable position, you're stuck with it for what can seem like an eternity. And if sitting itself becomes painful on the first day of a retreat, you're in for six hours of pain for the next three days.

I'd brought painkillers and ibuprofen gel to get me through if my ankle got worse but I was pleased to find it seemed to relax and didn't cause me any further concern. However my hips felt stiff and this was potentially more worrying. I sat in the kneeling position a few times and that helped, but kneeling put pressure on my ankles so it wasn't ideal.

I was usually alright for about twenty minutes and only the last five minutes of each sit were hard. I confess to allowing my mind to wander off and fantasise to distract myself. Why sit through pain when you can think about your favourite things, like karate? I knew the real reason I was feeling the pain was because I hadn't been sitting regularly enough. Previously, I'd attended Wednesday night sitting every week, doing a full hour each time. At home I'd been sitting for twenty minutes or half an hour a day. But recently I'd been distracted. I'd felt my karate training slipping and gone back to karate at the expense of zazen. Now I was paying the price.

By the last session of the day, I was beginning to wonder what was up with Tom. It was his job to ding the bell at the end of the session, but there was just a deafening silence. Had he nodded off on his cushion? Later, after the relief of the bell finally came, others said the same. The sit had seemed interminable. Tom assured us he hadn't been dozing, or missed the timer. Then the aches and pains were momentarily forgotten when Cathy, a teacher and talented singer-songwriter, said the Buddha had appeared before her. In Zen, we're told to ignore any visions that might occur while sitting, these are just fanciful notions bubbling up from the imagination. But Cathy insisted she really had seen the Buddha! Only after the bell, when she'd been able to turn around, had she seen the little statue on the window sill that had been casting a shadow on the wall.

During the talks and discussions, one message stood out for me. Mike urged us not to look for the meaning of Dogen's words in words but rather in experience. I tried to think what that means – which probably didn't help – but I knew there was something profoundly true and very important in this.

In martial arts we receive teachings all the time, not just from our sensei. We can pick up books and watch videos. We can research the training methods of the old masters and cross reference them with modern sports science. We can buy kettlebells and strap on fitbits. We can download apps and print off Navy SEAL training programmes. We can go on forums and get advice from martial artists all over the world. But all this time, we haven't done a single kick or punch.

It's not wrong, but so far we haven't accessed the most useful teacher of all – experience. We're in danger of learning from other people's experience, not our own. Nothing will teach you how to do push-ups on your knuckles better than doing push-ups on your knuckles. You will teach yourself that squeezing your fist tighter hurts less. You'll discover how strong you are. How many reps you can do. How many you can do if you do them properly. And how many you can do if you cheat. Eventually you'll learn that cheating makes you feel good about numbers in your head, but correct form means you hit harder and even the good fighters start to respect you. You learn which way delivers more in reality.

The trouble with much of the Zen writings, including Dogen's, is that they are beautiful and unusual and intriguing. They take us to a faraway land of mystery and wisdom, with Zen monks and samurai poets and temples on mist covered mountains. But real life is never elsewhere. It's always right here. So grubby and familiar that we barely bother to notice it. So ordinary that we yearn for something a little more extraordinary.

Dreaming of a different reality is what we do all the time. Wishing for this, and that, and the other. Wishing never changes anything, and wishing harder makes no difference either. In fact, the harder you wish, the further you stray from reality. But one action, no matter how small, is a step in the right direction.

It's not like there's no thinking in action. Action is not mindless. Fighting brilliantly is certainly not mindless. Performing a medal-winning kata is not mindless. It's simply that the thought is wholly contained in the action. It merges and disappears into the action. There is no wishing or dreaming. No judging or assessing. No consideration of good or bad. There is just mind and body, lost in action. In his final talk, Mike spoke of a poem that his teacher, Nishijima Roshi, had valued so highly that he'd used the opening line as a seal on his Certificates of Ordination. The line reads:

Seki Shin Hen Pen

Mike translated this literally as 'Red Mind, Slice, Slice'. (In case you're wondering why Hen and Pen are two different words for the same thing, it should be Hen, Hen, but the pronunciation of the second word is changed to avoid repetition. And if you're interested, the full poem and translation can be found in the Appendix.)

Mike explained that red means raw. Shin can be taken to mean mind/heart/consciousness – it doesn't refer to only the intellectual area, so Mike's preferred translation for 'seki shin' is 'unconditioned consciousness' or 'unconditioned awareness'. Slice by slice means moment by moment – each razor-thin slice of time that we consider a moment. The poem is an exhortation to live each and every moment with raw consciousness, uncooked, unseasoned, ungarnished. Untainted. It was a strong, simple image to take back to London with me.

NATURE PREACHES THE DHARMA

The peace of the recent retreat seemed far away as I returned to the daily grind. Making my way into central London each morning, I would hurry to get a seat on the tube so I could read my book in peace. My station's near the end of the line and the train travels over-ground for a few stops before disappearing into the tunnel. By this time, I'd disappeared into one of my commentaries on Dogen's writings and this would keep me engrossed until I reached my stop. I discovered a beautiful passage called 'Keisei Sanshiki', which translates as 'River Voices and Mountain Forms.' In it, a student visits the picturesque region of Lushan and hears a mountain stream flowing through the night. He gets inspired and writes a verse, which he presents to Zen master Joso:

The voices of the river valley are the Buddha's tongue,
The form of the mountains is nothing other than his
pure body,
Through the night, eighty-four thousand verses,
On another day, how can I tell them to others?

The master affirms the verse – signifying that the student has captured something of reality. In Gudo Nishijima's translation, Dogen refers to this as, 'the *non-emotional* preaching the Dharma'. Non-emotional means inanimate objects like mountains and streams, from nature, which is showing us reality all the time if we'd just care to look. Rather than using our minds to assess and research and chatter and process ideas about the nature of things, why not experience them directly? Simply see what's right in front of us.

The verse says that to experience the forms of the mountains directly is what the Buddha's teachings are all about. In this way, they 'embody' the Buddha. The sound of the stream is an opportunity to hear water bubbling just as it is, without filtering or processing. A chance to experience reality that goes on all night, never stopping, like 'Eight-four-thousand verses,' preaching the Dharma, just as the Buddha's tongue did.

In the first three lines, the student captures something ineffable in words and we feel we can glimpse what he's trying to get across. But in the last line he laments that when the night is over, it'll be hard to express what he has experienced to anyone else. In the cold light of day, how's he going to convey his experience to others? All he has is words, and words are not the same as experience. *You had to be there* – as they say.

There are several more instances in the chapter about nature, or natural events, revealing reality. A learned monk is put on the spot by his master and told to say something of his own. He can't think of a single word. He burns all his books and gives up trying to understand the Buddha-Dharma through learning, saying 'A picture of a rice cake can't stave off hunger'. He takes a job as a servant in the kitchen (doing something real) and asks the master to say something for him. But the master refuses, saying he could, but he (the student) would begrudge it later.

Finally, the student leaves the temple altogether and makes a living cultivating bamboo. One day while sweeping the path, a small piece of tile gets flicked up and strikes a bamboo stem. On hearing this sharp, hollow sound, he is 'snapped out' of his reverie (delusion) and into reality. He 'realises the great state of realisation' and returns to his master, saying, 'If you had explained it to me before, how would this thing have been possible? The depth of your kindness surpasses that of a parent.' It was only after the student had stopped seeking to understand reality in his mind, or trying to get someone else's version of it, that he was able to experience it for himself.

In another story, Zen Master Shigon has been seeking the truth for thirty years. One day, he sees peach blossoms in full bloom and composes this verse:

For thirty years, a traveller in search of a sword
How many times have leaves fallen and buds sprouted?
After one look at the peach blossoms
I have arrived directly at the present
And have no further doubts

The sword is a symbol of understanding that cuts through delusion. The peach blossoms were simply what was in front of Shigon at that moment. They were reality. He'd been seeking something 'other' all this time, but now he'd stopped seeking and was simply looking.

When you consider it, nature has been showing us reality ever since the first men stood and walked. The planets always went around the sun. The moon always affected the tides. Gravity never failed to pull things to earth. Nature was just as it was. But we believed the earth was flat, the sun went around the earth, and the sea somehow didn't spill off the edge. Nature continued to manifest reality, but we didn't interpret it correctly until a few enlightened men managed to convince us otherwise.

These men, now called geniuses: Galileo, Newton, Einstein and the like, were considered heretics in their time. They were ignored, ridiculed, even tortured, for suggesting that what we trusted and believed was the truth was only made-up patterns in our heads.

In karate, nature shows us the way to correct technique, but we rarely appreciate it. We push too much power and effort and noise through our work to feel the subtle hints that come from our surroundings and our relationship with the ground beneath us and the air around us. From the feedback of inanimate objects, like a punch-bag or makiwara (striking post).

To experience this feedback requires one thing above all else, and that is to 'forget' how you think you're supposed to move and allow yourself to experiment until you feel the most natural, balanced and powerful version of a technique.

In my own experience, it took fifteen years before I began to feel a natural connection at a basic level. And another fifteen before I began to feel it through and through. I used to want to speed up this learning for the students I was teaching but I've come to realise it can't be rushed. Bit by bit, it will happen. I've also learnt that effort, fitness, aggression and mind-set will, in truth, more than compensate for this lack of connection. However there comes a time to put all them aside and spend time just 'listening' to how your body connects to nature.

When that time has come, find a quiet place with a flat floor, somewhere you won't be disturbed. Before you can see, hear or feel your connection to nature, it helps to quieten the mind of your own thoughts that get in the way. So sit or kneel comfortably and make sure you have a firm base with three points on the ground. Sit upright, as if the crown of your head is being pulled up on a string. Move forward and back, left and right, until you find that sweet spot right in the centre. Then, holding this posture, relax a little and allow your body and mind to settle.

Put your attention into your sitting, your breath, your posture, and your environment. If other thoughts arise, usher them away and return to your sitting. Keep your attention present in each moment. Don't go wandering off into daydreams, worries or concerns. Stay present. Stay aware. It's a lot harder than it sounds, but just consider it training. The more you practise, the better you get.

Allow your mind to become aware of your posture, starting with your head. Relax any tension around your eyes or jawline. Soften the muscles in your neck and shoulders. Become aware of any tensions in your chest, back, or lower abdomen. If you feel a knot of tension, try to disband it, without slouching. Continue this sitting for five minutes and build up to fifteen minutes gradually. Then get up slowly and stand in your normal 'ready' position. This time work from the feet up. Imagine you've dipped your feet in ink and you're standing on paper to create a print. You need to get two perfect registers, that means every part of each foot, each toe, each edge and each heel, needs to be equally connected to the paper.

Press your feet into the paper by sinking your weight. Soften your knees and allow your body to rest heavy on the ground. Now perform a kata, very slowly – Tai Chi speed – and, with each turn, reprint your feet on the paper. After each step and turn, send your awareness into your feet and check how well they are registering. Notice if your big toe is off the paper, or your heel is pushing down too hard, or one side is printing heavier than the other. Correct the registration before you move on.

Here's an important point to keep in mind during this exercise. The aim is not to perfect this slow kata per se, but rather to allow this exercise to seep into your fast kata, your sparring, and the whole of your karate. Spend at least five minutes concentrating on foot-printing before taking your attention elsewhere.

Now you can perform your kata a little faster, but keep

your effort stripped back. You are trying to get feedback from your environment. Too much effort creates noise and you can't 'hear' over it. We're looking for feedback from the air around us and sensations in our own bodies. But be careful, because we're looking for a very elusive kind of feedback: the feedback of 'no feedback'. I probably need to explain! Try and think in terms of classic geometry and mechanics and make every movement a perfect straight line or a smooth circle. If a punch is straight, your fist and forearm should move forward like an arrow, and twist like a bullet. If an arrow is flying straight there's no wobbling. Similarly, if your punch is straight, your elbow should stay behind your fist. If you allow it to drift out it will create a wobble that you can feel.

That means you can feel the sensation of a wobbly technique far more than a true or straight technique. So, when it comes to feedback, less is more. Experiment over and over with your straight punches and strikes until you get the smoothest sensation in your delivery.

Use a circular movement of hips and shoulders to generate power around your vertical axis. This is the same axis that you established in your sitting. And with your feet evenly planted ('printed') you now have a perfect mechanical base from which to launch your strikes. Keep your elbow behind your hand and use body rotation rather than muscular effort.

Remember this is soft-training, and should be viewed as an enhancement to hard training, not a substitute. I recommend it as something you can do on rest days that allows your body to warm up gently and relax while it recovers from a harder session.

If you're training with weapons, they can give you excellent feedback. Take a stick and swing it. If you get a fast acceleration, and more importantly a straight path through the air, it will let you know with a 'whooshing' sound. You can get this whoosh with single or double sticks, short or long. Swing the stick across and back, experimenting until you get the sound. While you do have to hold the stick firmly to avoid dropping it (or throwing it through a window!) don't try and control it too tightly. Let the stick follow its own line and it will go faster.

Remember that while the stick itself is an inanimate object, it is still speaking to you, if you know how to listen. Try holding it in the centre and spinning it in a sideways figure 8 (infinity symbol). Once you get the stick moving around its central point, you'll feel how smoothly it travels. You'll get the feedback of no feedback. After five minutes, try some set movements or a stick kata and feel the difference after developing a connection with 'the non-emotional' – the inanimate stick, the air around you and the earth beneath your ink-stained feet.

EMPTY PAGES

The end of May is one of my favourite times of year. It's my dad's birthday, for a start, and we normally go up to Worcester for a visit. The weather is usually fine and the countryside looks fresh and green, filled with the promise of the summer to come. It was also the time to return to one of my all-time favourite places, Anam Cara, for our next three-day Zen retreat. This time, packing felt different. I knew what to expect and I found myself looking forward to the Highland landscapes and the friendly faces that would welcome me up there. I was taking only a small daypack so I left it late to pack. On the morning of the flight, I couldn't find my trusty Moleskine that I'd used to take notes at previous retreats and I was forced to bring a different notebook instead. This one had been given to me by a company that I didn't much like and their logo was printed big and bold on the front cover. Maybe this was why, when I got home after three days, there was nothing but blank pages inside.

That's not to say I learnt nothing noteworthy. Far from it. I'd felt the same awe that I always felt when Mike spoke. I was still moved by how he managed to capture things so simply. How he made the complicated seem clear. How his view made sense to me – sometimes overtly, and sometimes just a feeling that he was saying something true, but I couldn't quite grasp it. Like I was on a boat tour and the guide was describing a sight we were about to visit, but as we approached it, the place was shrouded in mist. I could make out a vague outline, and it was exciting, but I couldn't see it clearly. Not yet.

This time around, the whole retreat was calmer and more relaxed, with none of the fireworks that I remembered from last year's discussions. The silent eating still felt a little strange but it was no big deal. By the third day, I felt comfortable with the silence and less need to fill it with noise. Watching people eating, and serving, I began to try and understand my usual responses. Normally, if someone makes a mistake and everyone's watching, there's the urge to giggle. But this is nervous laughter – just one of our many conditioned responses. So someone spilt some porridge. So someone has a bit of egg around their mouth. So what? Someone's being human. I tried to be more accepting and it felt good to let go. To think, bless you, you clumsy oaf, because there but by the grace of God go I. Later, when Mike read a few lines from Genjo Koan – the passage I'd been studying like a kata – I was thrilled. We spoke about the line that says:

Setting out to make ourselves one with reality is delusion. Reality making ourselves part of it is waking up.

This idea of setting out to achieve enlightenment is sometimes translated as 'striving' or 'driving ourselves' to achieve an awakened state. We had an interesting discussion on the idea of trying. Is effort important? Surely we must be prepared to try and strive and work hard to achieve something worthwhile? It's true in most things, isn't it? Trying to do good. Trying to do the right thing. It must be true in an endeavour like karate, right? They put the question to me but I answered that I'm not a big fan of 'trying'. Trying is something you do when you're not sure. Or when you're not good at something. Mother tells Little

Johnnie, 'I know you struggle with maths but just try your hardest, that's all you can do.' This is good advice from a parent to a child, but it's not the right mind-set for a karate-ka who wants to win a fight or perform at the highest level. Watch the end of a long distance track race. As the leading athletes approach the final bend, the one at the front usually looks like he's trying the hardest. His face is screwed up in concentration and effort. The second one looks like he's running the hardest, his legs and arms are moving quickly. The third one looks composed and his stride is steady and even. He appears to be trying the least. But nine times out of ten, he will win. He's kept his composure and held his form for longer than the others. So when they hit the home straight, he has an extra gear as he kicks for the finish line. The important question is: who really tried the hardest? The first two runners gave it their all and didn't win. But did the winner 'not' try his hardest, or did his effort simply manifest in a different way? He remained composed. He held his form. He probably trained all season like this, and succeeded on the big day. But there's something more as well. He was third until the final lap, content to settle in behind the other two. He ran in their slipstream and used them as a target to hunt them down around the final bend. This 'hunter' mind-set had no thought for his own effort – he was too busy engaging in his racing. His effort was high, very high, perhaps he gave everything he had by the time he reached the finish line. But his 'trying' had disappeared into his doing, into the action of racing. And it's the same in karate.

When I'm coaching fighters, I tell them not to reveal their effort. If they look like they're trying too hard, their opponent will pick up on it. If they look like they're near their limit, the opponent will feed off this information. This is not to say that effort isn't important or necessary, of course it is. But all too often, the act of trying gets in the way of doing. This is what I take from Dogen's words.

After the first morning sitting, it was time for Samu (work) around the farm. I found myself with Mike and a woman I'd just met for the first time, Rachel. We were trimming back the grass on either side of the path that led to the meditation hall. I know, I know, it's almost too good to be true, but this wasn't an analogy, we really were clearing the way using real spades.

I'd only seen Mike once since the January Sesshin in Swindon and I was keen to hear him talk and to speak to him. In between seeing him, I always had hundreds of questions to ask, but whenever I did see him, I couldn't think of a single one. Sometimes they just disappeared from my mind and other times, they just felt a bit simple and lame and I had the feeling I knew how he'd react. He would pull his head back slightly and look down his long nose at me, frowning slightly to make sure he'd understood correctly, and then think for a few moments before answering. And as often as not, he'd give the answer that, in some way, I knew he'd give beforehand.

But this time there were no questions. Instead, we spent the best part of an hour talking about children. Rachel spoke a little about her daughter who'd returned from travelling the world, and I shared the happy news that I'd recently adopted a little girl. It struck me how easy it was to talk to Mike about real things, and how genuinely happy he seemed to hear about them.

Later in one of his talks, Mike told the story of a master reading a scroll. A student came by and asked him, 'Are you studying the scrolls?' The master answered, 'No, I'm just resting my eyes on them.' The student asked if he could do the same and the master told him, 'No, you'll burn a hole in them.'

The message is don't over-analyse the teachings or you'll destroy the benefit of reading them. Words are just words. Analogies are just analogies. Metaphors are just metaphors. They are not the same as reality, and never can be. As soon as you start analysing them and dissecting them they fall apart and lose their value.

Mike advised us to read Dogen in the same way that we might look at a painting. Let the words move us rather than settling down to analyse them to death. It's tempting to take words, phrases and sentences and examine them. If this word means this, then does that word mean that? If this is so, then does this mean that? Pretty soon we can make anything sound like nonsense. Like a good lawyer, we can turn any argument on its head. Like an online troll, we can unpick anything and make it seem stupid. But where does this leave us? Rather than following a direction, a suggestion, a 'finger, pointing', we examine the sign, the suggestion, the finger, endlessly, to see if we've understood it correctly. So we go nowhere. We move no further forward. The Buddha's teachings are often compared to a raft that gets us from one side to another – from delusion to awakening. But we keep checking the raft and picking holes in it. And what good is a raft with holes in it? We need to use the raft to make the journey and then forget about the raft.

Mike introduced his friend and long-time practitioner Ralph Hoyte to the rest of the group, calling him a Zen master (much to Ralph's embarrassment). Ralph is a poet and author and Mike asked him to read a poem about being a Buddhist. Or in this case, *not* being a Buddhist. I liked it so much that I asked Ralph if I could reproduce it, and he kindly agreed.

Not, by Ralph Hoyte

I am not a Buddhist, I am not;
I am a poet who (not all that often) does Zazen;
And moons circle around me,
Oh stars shine in on me;

I am not a Buddhist, not;
I eat meat, like women, sex;
Oh planets gyre in awakening dreams,
Birds bird through and vibrant in light;

I am a Buddhist, not;
I have no intention of keeping the precepts,
No intention;

Don't know when the Buddha's birthday is
(Didn't get invited to the party),
Cannot recite the sutras forwards or backwards,
but know them inside out;
I am not, am;
So long ago: 'Ralph?'
'Yes?' So I have to give that up, too;
Yet it's alright to be Ralph;

I am not a Buddhist, mu!
The Buddha was not a Buddhist, boo!
I do not know what I am,
Do not know what I will do next,
I alone am uncatchable and leave no trace,
No path, no way, no middle;
A path, a way, a middle: Go! Ask!

Blackbird trills, snail slimes,
The children quarrel,
My wife tells me off;
I am not a Buddhist
(He's such a Buddhist);
Ask me, I will say:

Something in Ralph's words resonated with me. The feelings he was expressing about his practice mirrored my own. That on/off sense of trying and failing, and trying again. Never quite feeling able to do it perfectly. Never quite ready to give up. It seems to be the same for

Buddhists and martial artists. Our practice leads us in a merry dance alright. Descriptions of reality are only post-its or snapshots pieced together like a photo-montage. They are clunky and incomplete. A skilful artist can capture something of reality, but it's never the whole picture. Reading a passage from Dogen and trying to understand the whole of reality is like looking at a painting by Cezanne and trying to understand France.

Dogen wrote 95 chapters trying to capture something of the ineffable Dharma. But each one is just a hint or a flavour rather than the whole thing. Just as, even if you could see every French painting from the early cave painters to the impressionists, expressionists and modern masters, you would not have a complete picture of France. Throw in every photograph, video and film, every book and word written, and you could easily find plenty that's still missing. France is too big to capture completely in any form of description. And too small. Because even if you could somehow capture the complete country, then you'd be missing the tiny details and the smallest atoms and molecules that still exist as parts of France. So don't overthink things. Take a flavour or resonance from the message and let it move you and inspire you.

In karate, don't overthink your upper block. Do it the way you're shown until it's time to change. When is the right time to change? Your instructor will tell you. Or you will know. The truth is that nothing in this whole world is fixed forever. Any definition or way of doing things will always, ultimately, be subject to change. So don't get too upset by this. Keep things fixed until it's time to change. Then change. Be like Dogen and return from China with a flexible mind.

NO MIND

Think back to your last big test. If you're a martial artist, it could be your last grading but it could equally be something from everyday life like an important presentation, a concert, a job interview – it doesn't really matter. What does matter is that you put yourself on the spot and you were forced to perform. You did so because you considered the rewards worth it. You wanted a new belt. You wanted to reach a new level. But the pitfalls were also lurking on the side-lines: pain, tiredness, fear, failure, ridicule.

Go back a little further, to the time leading up to the test. That time when you tell yourself to relax, but you can't. You try and make a cup of tea but your hand is shaking. You need to eat to keep your strength up but you're not hungry. You're having trouble keeping anything down. People wish you luck, but you know luck has nothing to do with it. You reply, but you're not listening. Not really. You're already on the field, on the stage, on the mat, on the track, on the spot. Your field of vision narrows and your hearing begins to filter out all unnecessary sounds. Even your own voice sounds far away.

Now, in the hours and minutes and seconds leading up to

the moment of truth – those hours and minutes and seconds that seem to go on forever, stretched out by some malevolent force that wants you to suffer far longer than necessary – you're experiencing the biggest test of all. *Before* the test.

Because now you still have the chance to bow out gracefully. You're not well. You have an injury. A family matter, of some delicacy, suddenly arisen, out of the blue. A reason why you shouldn't do it. One you can't believe you hadn't considered before. Such a good reason that you can't possibly ignore it and everyone will certainly understand. And yet… you've lived just long enough to know that if you give in to this reason now, you'll feel bad later. You'll regret it. And over time, that regret will feel far worse than the upset you're feeling now.

And because of your stubborn insistence to go ahead with this stupid, unnecessary and totally ridiculous idea you had a while back, you find yourself stepping up and the test is beginning. The nerves are welling up like ocean swells threatening to capsize you and it's all you can do to keep upright in the water.

The test begins and immediately, it's painfully apparent you shouldn't be here. You should have made your excuses. You will never be able to do this. You plod on, cursing your own stupidity for putting yourself in this situation.

From the start, the pace is brutal. The warm-up feels more like an endurance test than a gentle build up. The others around you look grim and determined and you feel you're falling behind. You know you won't be able to keep up for much longer. Eventually you warm up and settle into things a little. You perform your set pieces without any big problems. But as time goes on, you're starting to feel deep-down tiredness. The mental nerves and physical exhaustion combine and collide and make your hands and limbs weigh heavy on you. And now, at your most tired, you're called upon to face your most difficult opponents. One after another they come out and you fight.

Some say you go into autopilot but that's not quite true, you're still thinking. You're not just reacting like an automaton. You're using some strategy and tactics to give yourself an advantage. Parts of you are acting automatically, repeating drilled techniques, but others are capable of being fluid, subtle and changing to suit whatever conditions arise.

You are aware of everything – the opponent, the arena, the crowd, the instructors, your own body – but you're not fixed on any one thing. Now, in this moment of greatest pressure – the moment that caused you all that anguish in the run-up – your stomach isn't doing somersaults and you don't feel sick or uneasy. Don't get me wrong, you don't feel great either. You're not on cloud nine and floating in nirvana. But you're not suffering mental turmoil. Not now. Not anymore. Not one drop.

Why is that? Because you're no longer thinking in isolation. You're acting. Your hands and feet are blocking and striking. Even that opponent you didn't want to face can't seem to hurt you now. Well, not too badly anyway.

The noise of the crowd, the scrutiny of the instructors, the danger of getting knocked out, teeth broken, nose smashed – they are all present, but they don't bother you.

How to describe this state? In English we have several words that touch on it. You're 'in the flow' or 'in the zone'. No matter what level you are, beginner or black belt, if you're fighting this way, you're a force to be reckoned with. A fighter who's wholeheartedly engaged is difficult to put away. If you were a football team, you'd be playing to your full potential. Each player would be doing his part and contributing to the whole game. Playing like this, a team is said to be more than the sum of its parts. But in reality, it's simply playing to its full capacity, which teams so rarely do. You're Leicester City shocking the world to win the Premier League.

How does your mind enter this state in the midst of such a difficult test? It begins with giving the task undivided attention. Once the mind is wholly engaged, the body and mind become one. Every thought and muscle and sinew and nerve-signal works in unison. While you're acting in this way, your mind isn't stopping to discriminate between punching or blocking, kicking or sweeping. There's no pause to consider whether doing something is a good idea or a bad idea, because you know pausing is a very bad idea. Just 'doing' is a better option. There's no right or wrong now because what's done is done, and the results are already happening. If your action created an opportunity, you take it. If your action gave your opponent an opening, you deal with it. There's still no time to stop and consider whether what you did was right or wrong. Because you know stopping is wrong. When all eleven football players are working together, they are playing at their best. But what happens when one thinks he can improve things by stepping off the pitch and onto the side-lines to see what's going on? Instead of marking his man, he's running up and down offering helpful advice to his teammates. And while he's doing this, another player decides he doesn't agree with the advice and leaves the pitch to start arguing. Now while these two tossers are trying to work out what's wrong and how to win, the team is down to nine men. How much better off was everyone when the whole team was engaged in the game?

Of course, someone's still in charge. The team needs a captain and guess what – it has one. One part of your brain is thinking and responding, keeping an eye on the bigger picture, while the rest is taking care of other business. But that controlling and guiding part must remain engaged in the game – a player-captain, not a manager or coach.

I did a little research into some of the most successful football captains, hoping to find something that united them. Perhaps it was some sort of great strategic insight, or incredible skill, or iron will? But the names that came up were as varied as their abilities and personalities. Some were famous for their dedication and work ethic like Bobby Moore, John Terry and Steve Gerrard, but others were renowned for their skill and flair, names like Eric Cantona, Diego Maradona and Michel Platini. It seemed there was no singular personality or style required to being a great captain. The word used most often in all cases was 'inspiration'. These captains led by example. Their wholehearted commitment to the game inspired their teammates to do likewise. They did this, not from the side-lines, but from their own deep involvement in the game as it played out. They became the embodiment of the whole team in one player, and succeeded in unifying the team to play as one.

Of course, there is a time to stop and assess, to analyse and coach, to discuss and argue. But that time is in training. When you're playing, just play. When you're performing, just perform. When you're fighting, just fight. And when you're assessing, just assess.

If you're 'holding a thought' it's like playing with a burden, like carrying a heavy bag that's only going to get in the way and obstruct you. Don't bring any preconceived ideas with you. You're free to access your entire mind and knowledge as you need it – on the fly. It hasn't disappeared or gone anywhere. It's simply not blocking you from what you need to do right now.

When you're wholly engaged in an activity… fighting, playing, performing… your mind and body become one and blend with your surroundings. In a way, you become one with your opponent, your team, your environment.

This undivided whole is as good as it gets and it's this 'wholly-engaged mind' that's known in the martial arts as Mushin. The usual translations of 'No Mind' or 'Empty Mind' are both quite misleading. I much prefer 'Unfettered Mind,' because this implies a mind free of preconceptions, open to all possibilities in every moment. I used the example of fighting in a grading to highlight an important irony. A mind can often be in turmoil before a difficult event, and yet unperturbed in the heat of it. This had been my own experience towards the end of my own biggest test – the 30 Man Kumite – where I felt most calm and serene in the greatest storm of the test.

I have written in-depth about this experience in my book Waking Dragons and I have seen karate fighters of all grades go through similar, whether they know it or not. At some point in the test they seem to 'forget themselves' and simply do what they need to do. They become one with the action required and blend with the opponent, instead of clashing. They feel tiredness and pain but neither bother them unduly nor hinder their performance.

It's important to realise that they don't become superhuman or achieve any special powers. They are simply performing at their best, in concert with themselves. It seems our consciousness can overcome inner turmoil even in the direst circumstances and find a serene state, just by doing something other than 'thinking'. The good news is we don't always need a high pressure situation to achieve this. In fact, we achieve it all the time. The key is that it is achieved in action. This action doesn't have to be in sport or martial arts. It helps if what you're doing is engrossing, which is why arts and crafts are useful ways to enter this state. Casting clay on a wheel, daubing paint on a canvas, playing an instrument, gardening, woodwork, cooking, cleaning. If you consider these simple activities, they unite body and mind in action. There is the need for some concentration and consideration, some thought and indeed some emotion and care about what you're doing. These are all activities that can feel quite therapeutic. When performing these simple actions, our consciousness is given a break from pure thinking – from constructing a series of abstract forms and concepts that are unrelated to what the rest of the body is doing. Instead of forming concepts, it is re-engaged in what it does most naturally, which is 'doing'.

In Buddhist terms, the idea of returning to this state has many names: Original Mind, Beginner's Mind, Buddha Nature or Original Face, a balanced state between thinking, feeling and doing that unfolds moment by moment. In this state there is no worry about whether you can or can't do something. No consideration about how you feel, whether you feel good or bad about your situation. It's more than simply enabling your best performance, it's equally about eliminating the stories we tell ourselves all the time and the inner turmoil they produce, based on nothing more than the imagination. These stories plague our lives so much more than they should. In his book 'Sit Down and Shut Up,' Brad Warner puts it bluntly, and brilliantly:

Real wisdom is the ability to understand the incredible extent to which you bullshit yourself every single moment of every day.

KARATE ON A CUSHION

The karate grading is just one example. You told yourself a dozen good reasons why you should pull out. But fortunately, you had just enough awareness to ignore these whispers and go ahead anyway. You started out nervous, shaky, a bit stiff. Not your best. But somewhere along the way you warmed to the task and then you were fine. Maybe you were even on fire, flying, brilliant. Or maybe you were nothing special, you were just you. Happy enough just doing what you were doing. Not wanting anything different or anything more. Not wishing you were anywhere else. Even in the thick of the fighting, you just got on with it.

This is quite an achievement, don't you think? To find a sense of inner peace in the eye of the storm. But could this be something more. Could it actually be nirvana?

Surely nirvana is something far more blissful and wonderful. Yet the literal translation of nirvana is 'extinguishing'. Like putting out a fire. Like quenching a thirst. Like losing the desire to be somewhere else, doing something else. No longer dreaming of living a different life to the one you have.

What if nirvana is being happy enough with what you have right now? With what you're doing right now? Knowing that, by and large, you're responsible for where you are – and being okay with that. It doesn't sound anything like as special as it should. But this version of nirvana has one important quality that the happy-clappy blissful version doesn't. It sounds like something you can have right now, and any time you like, if you want it.

THE REAL DRAGON

In Fukanzazengi – Dogen's famous passage on how to sit in zazen – he writes: *I beseech you, noble followers of Zen, do not become so accustomed to images that you are dismayed by the real dragon.* What is the real dragon, in our lives, today? Not some beautiful or terrifying mythical beast that we fantasise about, but something far more scary: real life.

In his book, To Meet the Real Dragon, Master Nishijima writes: *A priest asked his master, 'What is Buddhism?' The master replied, 'To wear clothes and eat meals.' Another master said, 'Buddhism is carrying water for your cooking. It is gathering wood to build a cooking fire.' These words have no hidden meaning. They express the fundamental attitude of Buddhism directly. True Buddhism is everyday life itself.*

When I first read this passage, I loved the imagery: wearing clothes and eating meals, carrying water and gathering wood. It sounded so simple and real, but no sooner had I read these words than my mind began to wonder what ultimate truth they expressed. I began to search for metaphors, symbolism, allegory. Until I read the next line. *These words have no hidden meaning.* I felt like the town drunk in the old Westerns who gets a bucket of water in the face. The masters were talking about everyday life. Not life as we wish it could be, or imagine it should be. Not as it could be, or should be. But as it is. Good in places, bad in places. Nothing more, nothing less. Not living in the past. Not dreaming of a brighter future. Just attending to what we're doing, right now.

This acceptance of the situation we're in right now doesn't have to be passive. If we find ourselves in a crappy situation, we're free to try and change it. But we must also be realistic. We must also accept that our actions will have consequences. We must be honest with ourselves and accept the part we played in getting to where we are. Someone else may not be entirely to blame! We must be clear that no amount of wishing or wanting will change our situation one iota. But one small step will be a move in the right direction.

I saw a video recently of a speech by a former US admiral urging us to make our beds in the morning. This simple act was drummed into him in SEAL training and, he says, set the tone for everything else throughout the day. A small, simple, achievable action. Not a lot of thought required, just enough to get the sheets flat and the corners neat. But a good habit to get into from the first moment of the day.

This kind of advice is easy to give but harder to follow. Why? Because we've been conditioned, over the years, to use our minds for everything and think before we act. This is no bad thing in many ways, but it can easily become an obstacle. Thinking about doing something for any length of time is guaranteed to bring up a whole load of good reasons to avoid it. This can get in the way of achieving something meaningful or wonderful. Or doing something tedious but important, like the dishes, the laundry, the finances. Like making your bed.

I'm reminded of the time I began training in Sensei Gavin's dojo. I'd been studying with master Chris Rowen for some years and I'd enjoyed Chris's lectures on Zen and Japanese martial arts. Gavin's style had been quite different and he'd focused on pragmatic karate. His stories, usually recounted over a Guinness, tended to relate to door-work and self-protection. But then, at the end of yet another tough sweat session, he said something that convinced me the odd pearl of wisdom could fall from his lips, too. He told us the real secret to achieving great things in the martial arts. He said, *'The secret of training is training.'*

This simple statement sums up all you need to know about mastering karate. Over the years, it has become a recurring theme for us and a bit of a standing joke. After all, it's so obvious that it doesn't really need saying – does it? And yet as teachers, Gavin and I get hundreds of students asking about training, and telling us about training, and talking about training. But we can see the people who really are putting in the hours, and they're too busy to talk about it. When the tough moments come, as they invariably do, these people's training speaks for itself, louder than any words.

The founder of our karate style, Master Chojun Miyagi, lamented that he felt he was groping in the dark with karate. But he also offered this more positive conclusion: *'If we go forward to find the truth of karate with all our strength of mind and body, we will be rewarded little by little, day by day.'*

The reward is not somewhere in the future. It *is* the training. Put another way, training is its own reward. This is something I've come to appreciate as I grow older and perhaps even a tiny bit wiser. Rather than looking for karate to lead me to somewhere new, I've come to appreciate what it does for me right now. The strengthening of the body. The beauty of technique. The chance to switch off from daily concerns and focus on something completely different. To train with amazing people. A good night's sleep. These are all things I get from karate, by doing karate.

And from Zen? From Dogen's writings, and the practice of zazen that he recommends so strongly? Nothing very special. Just something so simple and obvious that we don't even think about it. A confirmation of what I already know from karate. The simple truth that to engage wholeheartedly in each exercise is the right way to do things. To listen wholeheartedly to a good teacher. To do as he says. Not as I think he says. Not as I think it should be done. But literally: *as he says*. This wholehearted engagement means we collect every ounce of benefit from each thing we do. Every bit of power and learning and technique is all taken on board instead of slipping through our fingers.

If the slightest gaps open, if the mind wanders and the posture wavers, then the technique goes and instead of training one hundred percent in the correct way we're training half-heartedly. Worse still, we're ingraining poor practice which takes a lot of time and effort to undo.

This goes beyond physical effort. It is complete effort that includes a high level of attention and care. Listening, watching, observing. Being completely honest with yourself at all times. Setting aside the ego, and thereby opening yourself up to everything – all the things you may be doing badly, as well as all the things you can do well.

Start training in this way from the moment you bow into the dojo and hold onto it for as long as you can. Over time, it will come naturally to you and there will be little you can't achieve. Better still, you'll enjoy your journey every step of the way.

KARATE ON A CUSHION

After penning the previous chapters, I set them aside for some time to percolate and see whether there was anything more I needed to add. Then I got busy with work and before I knew it, a year had gone by.

Reading them back now, I feel I said everything I wanted to say, probably more times than was strictly necessary, but I had to be sure! I hope I've conveyed that Zen and martial arts aren't really separate roads, or even two lanes on a dual carriageway. Rather, there are elements of one in the other, if we look closely. Kata is sometimes called 'moving meditation' and its practice can certainly produce a similar effect to meditation – a settled, 'rooted' feeling, a relaxed energy flowing through the body and a mind free of chatter and concern – at least for a while. And zazen is, in essence, karate exercises like breathing, posture, awareness and focus distilled into a single practice. Both challenge body and mind and both require a high degree of persistence and honesty to bring any deep-rooted change.

If I'm being honest, I haven't attended the Dogen Sangha regularly in the last year, nor sat for such long periods at home. Instead, I've tried to integrate meditation into my karate and my life in other ways, with fifteen minutes here and there, perhaps before training at home, or half an hour on the way to work. I've stopped reading on the train, not because I've become anti-intellectual, but because I can feel the impact it has on my neck and my posture, and posture is something I'm working on at the moment. I spend most of the day hunched over a keyboard, which is bad enough without also gazing down at a book. So instead, I practise standing meditation on the daily commute. I begin by establishing an upright posture and relaxing my shoulders, one at a time. The right shoulder takes a little longer than the left so it goes first and I change at Tufnell Park.

By the time we reach Euston my posture feels good so I work on my breathing. When I'm walking along the platform and someone gets in my way, I breathe, slow and deep. When someone cuts me up with a wheelie bag, I breathe, slow and deep. When someone stops at the top of the escalator to check their phone and I feel the rage rising up from the pit of my stomach, I breathe, slow and deep.

Unsurprisingly, I get to work feeling pretty good, and I go home the same way – doing something physical instead of filling my head with nonsense from books about Zen and martial arts. You should try it, once you've finished this book, of course.

I've kept in touch with Mike and the others at the Dogen Sangha by attending the longer Sesshin retreats. But these are few and far between and recently, I began to notice a certain restlessness in myself that prevented me from sitting at all. I found myself coming up with all sorts of excuses and 'more pressing concerns' that needed my attention. Underneath it all, I sensed I was missing that subtle stillness that comes from zazen.

There was only one thing for it – I returned to the Wednesday night sitting to reconnect with the Sangha and draw strength and resolve from the group. Tom was there, as he always is, to unlock the door and set out the mats, with his trusty clock and singing bowl arranged neatly in the corner. Matt was there too, distributing the cushions and showing newcomers how to sit in the correct posture. Other familiar faces appeared and we chatted quietly and stretched gently until, with everything arranged just so, we entered the zendo and walked in a dignified manner to our respective stations.

I found myself settling quickly onto my cushion and feeding off the quiet determination of the group to sit together in zazen. No 'more pressing concerns' came to mind and at that moment, there was nowhere I'd rather be and nothing else I'd rather be doing. I was just sitting on my cushion and attending to my posture and my breathing, happy to be doing just that and blissfully unaware of any little black dot (or was it a grubby little black mark?) that may or may not have been on the wall.

APPENDIX – SEKI SHIN HEN PEN

The poem is presented with literal translations for the reader to interpret.

21   Eihei Koroku Vol. 10 No. 21

Sekishin Red mind
henpen piece by piece
manten whole sky/heavens/universe
u exist

Jikini Directly
semmu thousand dreams
ichikaku one awakening/realisation
e kitaru (I) have got

Koutai Whole body
imada not yet
mei clear
san three (treasures)
hachi eight (fold path)
kyu nine (divisions of sutras)

Hitotabi One time
gisai have doubt
owatte finished
hitotabi one time
gisai have doubt

RECOMMENDED READING

The following books are listed by category and roughly in order of relevance and ease of reading to help you get started if you're new to the subject.

ZEN AND MARTIAL ARTS

When Buddhists Attack
Jeffrey K. Mann

Jeffrey Mann does a great job of laying out the history of Buddhism and Zen and its links to the martial arts. Thoroughly researched and widely referenced, it's definitely the place to start, and the hardback edition makes a handsome addition to any martial arts library.

Zen in the Martial Arts
Joe Hyams

A little dated now, but still an interesting perspective from someone who trained with Bruce Lee.

The Zen Teaching of Bodhidharma
Red Pine

A succinct insight into the Bodhidharma legend and some of the sutras he may have written or taught. Nothing much about martial arts, but a good insight into the man, and more importantly the thinking behind the study of the Way.

ZEN BUDDHISM

Buddhism Plain and Simple
Steve Hagen

A great place to start. This book has been around for some time but on rereading it recently, I was struck again by how good it is. The essence of Buddhism is simplicity itself but all too often, books on Buddhism can be anything but. Steve Hagen writes succinctly with great verve and manages to make things really clear.

Books by Brad Warner

Brad Warner is an interesting character, an American Zen master who's also a punk guitarist and Godzilla fan. Brad studied with Gudo Nishijima Roshi for many years and received Dharma transmission from him. His books are written in a very accessible way that doesn't take Zen too seriously, and get their meaning across all the better for it. Below are the three books I've read – I imagine the rest are equally good:

1. Hardcore Zen
2. Sit Down and Shut Up
3. Don't Be a Jerk

Zen Mind, Beginner's Mind
Shunryu Suzuki

A classic, and deservedly so. Shunryu Suzuki went to San Francisco in 1959 to lead the Japanese Soto Zen school and ended up staying for 12 years. He became a beloved teacher and inspired many modern day American writers and practitioners. Reading 'Zen Mind, Beginner's Mind,' will tell you why.

To Meet the Real Dragon
Gudo Nishijima

I wouldn't have discovered this gem without visiting the Dogen Sangha in London. Gudo Nishijima was Mike Luetchford's teacher for many years and also taught Brad Warner. Master Nishijima is very much his own thinker and he offers a rather unique perspective on Zen. Years of looking to the West, teaching Westerners and researching Western thought have added a level of insight that resonates with a Western reader. This, coupled with over fifty years of studying Dogen, makes for an enlightening read.

Eat, Sleep, Sit
Kaoru Nonomura

A first-hand account of a Japanese salaryman's experience at Eiheiji, the temple founded in the 13th century by Dogen that still operates today. The place has a reputation for strictness and austerity and little has changed since Dogen first penned his 'Rules for the Cloud Hall.' An interesting read but ultimately, more about the outward appearance of Zen than the inner core.

DOGEN'S WRITING

There are several books featuring selected chapters from Dogen's masterwork, the Shobogenzo. These are recommended as a good introduction to Dogen and the core of his writing without wading through the entire work, which is truly a heavy task.

Moon in a Dewdrop
Zen Master Dogen – edited by Kazuaki Tanahashi

Beyond Thinking – A Guide to Zen Meditation
Zen Master Dogen – edited by Kazuaki Tanahashi

Shobogenzo – Zen Essays by Dogen
Translated by Thomas Cleary

Realising Genjo Koan
Shohaku Okamura

This is a whole book dedicated to one chapter of Dogen's Shobogenzo, the famous Genjo Koan. The meaning is made wonderfully clear by Shohaku Okamura – a very talented writer and teacher.

The Mountains and Waters Sutra
Shohaku Okamura

Another whole book dedicated to one chapter of the Shobogenzo. I found it a little more difficult to follow than his other book 'Realizing Genjo Koan' but worthy of another read soon, I feel.

Shobogenzo 1, 2, 3 and 4
Nishijima/Cross

This complete translation is split across 4 volumes, with extensive notes. It's a lifetime's work from Gudo Nishijima and an incredible achievement, however not one to be entered lightly. I'd recommend selected works first to get the hang of Dogen's style before venturing into the full four volumes.

Master Dogen's Shinji Shobogenzo
Gudo Nishijima
Edited by Mike Luetchford and Jeremy Pearson

A selection of 301 koans from Dogen's collection, complete with commentary on each. A great way to get to grips with how to appreciate Zen koans.

Between Heaven and Earth
Mike Luetchford

This translation of the Indian master Nagarjuna's writing makes for some pretty dense material, however Mike's commentary in between chapters adds clarity and some fascinating insight into the connection between Dogen and Nagarjuna.

BRAIN SCIENCE

Science, and in particular neuro-science, is always making new headway in understanding the inner workings of the human mind and body. Perhaps a little surprisingly, with each new revelation, Buddhists often get to say, 'I told you so!' Here are two books that correspond quite closely with the Buddhist viewpoint, showing how the ancient Buddhists' understanding of how we think and perceive the world is being confirmed by modern scientists:

The Brain
David Eagleman

The Idiot Brain
Dean Burnett

ONLINE RESOURCES

TheZenSite.com

Search 'Dogen teaching' for plenty of great reference on the great man, including eight versions of Genjo Koan with side-by-side comparisons.

LondonZen.org and Shobogenzo.net

Articles and downloads from the writings of Gudo Nishijima Roshi and Mike Eido Luetchford.

ACKNOWLEDGEMENTS

I would like to thank Mike Luetchford sincerely for his guidance and support, and for sharing his wisdom and insights so freely in his teachings; Tom Brodie and Matt Greenshields for sharing their knowledge and experience so patiently each week; Ralph Hoyte for his companionship on retreats and for permission to reproduce his poem, 'Not'; and the whole of the Dogen Sangha for being such great company to sit with, and such fine sparring partners in discussions.

Despite the saying, a book *is* judged by its cover, so a big 'thank you' to my talented friend and fellow karate-ka Ben Hung for his illustration and design, I love the results. And I'm very grateful to my trusty team of readers, proofers and critics: my dear wife Charmaigne, my sensei Gavin Mulholland, my sister Sasha and my friends Frances Little, Jake Hoban and Mike Thornton – thank you for your valuable time and input.

NON-FICTION BY
GORAN POWELL

WAKING DRAGONS

The Thirty Man Kumite is one of karate's toughest tests, reserved for senior black belts with years of experience. One person fights a line-up of thirty fighters, one after another, full contact, moving up the grades to face the strongest, most dangerous fighters last. *Waking Dragons* is a true account of Goran Powell's Thirty Man Kumite and the lifetime of martial arts that led up to it. He covers the fitness training and mental preparations required for such a brutal test, talking openly of the conquest of fear and the spiritual growth that is at the heart of the traditional martial arts.

One of those rare books that you want to keep reading because it's so good, but fear reaching the end because then it will be over
Waterstones

Quite simply, this book is impossible to put down
Traditional Karate Magazine

An exciting and tense read with lots of action
Martial Arts Magazine

The author's journey is one in which we can find great wisdom, information that all martial artists should know
Lawrence Kane

It inspired me, and I know it will inspire you
Geoff Thompson

Shines a light into the darkest reaches of your psyche
Graham Wendes

While he relays the fight sequences in almost terrifyingly brutal detail, what really hits you is the real battles are won and lost in the mind
Doug Wood

EVERY WAKING MOMENT

Since recording his own 30 Man Kumite in his first book 'Waking Dragons' Goran has coached many fighters through one of karate's toughest tests. Fighting as Fight 30 at the end of the line, he also got a unique personal insight into the effectiveness of his own methods.

Every Waking Moment goes deep into the mental, physical and spiritual training required to face 30 hardened fighters, with chapters on advanced concepts like Chi, Yin, Yang and Tao, martial principles and strategy from The Art of War.

With a foreword by Gavin Mulholland and insights from successful fighters, Every Waking Moment reaches beyond the 30 Man Kumite to all aspects of karate and life outside the dojo walls.

Goran Powell has taken the craft of writing and storytelling and made it art.
Kris Wilder

In this truly remarkable book, Goran not only talks about the 30 Man, he lays out how to face it; how to prepare for it and ultimately, how to pass it.
Gavin Mulholland

Having been a part of the 30 man line-up for the last six years, I can personally attest to the effectiveness of the physical and mental training methods described
Danny Williams

Passages as heart-pounding and as well written as any action thriller… an effortless read, one that draws you on and on, with a 'just one more page' quality that is hard to find in a novel, let alone a book like this.
Richard Revell, Waterstones

Exceeding the lofty standard set by Powell's prior books, this is one of the finest tomes on karate available.
Lawrence Kane

AWARDS

Writer of the Year, British Martial Arts Awards 2017

FICTION BY GORAN POWELL

CHOJUN – A NOVEL

A typhoon brings the renowned karate master Chojun Miyagi into the life of young Kenichi Ota, who must prove himself before he can enter the master's inner circle. As once-peaceful Okinawa prepares for war, master and student venture to China in search of the deepest meaning of karate.

After Pearl Harbour, the tides of war turn against Japan and an American invasion fleet approaches. Kenichi is conscripted as a runner for the Japanese general staff and finds himself in the epicentre of the Battle of Okinawa. In the aftermath, he must fight again to rebuild the shattered hopes of his people and preserve his master's art.

Riveting, highly recommended – Lawrence Kane

Remarkable, it's that good! – Kris Wilder

Goran Powell has a marvellous way of capturing the tone of Asian storytelling – Loren W Christensen

Covers the relationship between student and Sensei beautifully – Nick Hughes

An exciting step in the evolution of how karate's history is told – Mike Clarke

Detailed, meticulously researched and absolutely compelling – Geoff Thompson

Enthralling… hard to put down – Violet Li

AWARDS

Winner: Eric Hoffer Award
Silver: Benjamin Franklin, Historical Fiction
Bronze: eLit Awards
Finalist: Book of the Year, ForeWord Magazine
Finalist: International Book Award
Finalist: British Martial Arts Awards 2016

A SUDDEN DAWN – FICTION

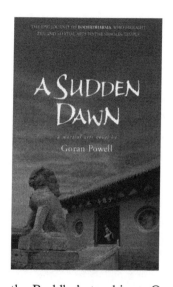

The life of Bodhidharma is steeped in myth and legend, 'A Sudden Dawn' is one version of his story. Born to the warrior caste, Bodhidharma gives up a glorious future as a soldier to become a monk and seek enlightenment. After years of searching in vain, he becomes enlightened in a single moment.

He accepts a mission to travel to China and spread the Buddha's teachings. On the way he meets an unlikely disciple, a Chinese fugitive named Ko. Together they venture to the Emperor's palace in Nanjing and beyond, to a temple in the mountains, Shaolin. But there are powerful forces at work to destroy the Indian master, and Ko's violent past catches up with him at the temple gate where a deadly reckoning must take place.

The book martial artists have been waiting 2000 years for Chris Crudelli, Mind Body & Kickass Moves

Bridges the gap between training and spirituality. Fabulously entertaining – Combat Magazine

Destined to become an epic tale of the warrior's journey
Patrick McCarthy

Inspirational, beautifully written, I loved it
Geoff Thompson

Weaves fact and fiction to produce a powerhouse of a page turner – Iain Abernethy

You can feel the hot breath of battle on your neck and the cool of the temple's damp hallways on your legs
Kris Wilder

As good as James Clavell's 'Shogun' – Lawrence Kane

Superbly crafted characters, surges with action
Loren W. Christensen

Walk alongside one of mankind's greatest legends
Gavin Mulholland

AWARDS

Winner: USA Book News, Historical Fiction 2010
Gold: eLit 2011, Gold: IP LivingNow 2011

MATRYOSHKA – COLD WAR THRILLER

The deadly arts of Soviet special forces are not lost, they have simply adapted to the new world order. Eva was once a soldier of the Cold War, trained in seduction and espionage, known as a 'Matryoshka' (Russian Doll). Today she is an art dealer in London but beneath the outer shell the Matryoshka is still at work.

When an operation goes wrong she is traced by a ghost from her past, her instructor Vasili Dimitriev. Dimitriev is hunting a traitor in Moscow. But the traitor has sent an Alpha team to silence both of them. As British police and the CIA close in, Eva and Vasili must work together in the deadliest game of all, where trust is weakness and love is a weapon.

Spies, Soviets, London…fighting! Treat yourself, you will enjoy – Kris Wilder

The author's knowledge of combat skills shines through
Gary Chamberlain

I can't help feeling Goran must have lived (impossible) in all the cities and times he sets Matryoshka in to bring them to life the way he does
Stuart Williams

The author's intimate understanding of combat makes the scenes so vivid, it's like watching a Hollywood action movie – Simon Clinch

The depth and intrigue of Homeland, and set with a Cold War background – Tim Clark

An engrossing action thriller from cover to cover, I couldn't put it down – Mike Thornton

ABOUT THE AUTHOR

Goran Powell is an award-winning freelance writer and martial artist who holds a 5th dan in Goju Ryu Karate. He works in London and teaches and trains at Daigaku Karate Kai, one of the UK's strongest clubs.

For more visit **goranpowell.com**

Printed in Poland
by Amazon Fulfillment
Poland Sp. z o.o., Wrocław

24888615R00125